JACOBIT
PERTHSHIRE
1745

by

Frances McDonnell

CLEARFIELD

Printed for
Clearfield Company, Inc. by
Genealogical Publishing Co., Inc.
Baltimore, Maryland
1999

Reprinted for
Clearfield Company, Inc. by
Genealogical Publishing Co., Inc.
Baltimore, Maryland
2002

International Standard Book Number: 0-8063-4838-0

Made in the United States of America

Introduction

The reign of the House of Stuart came to an end in 1689 when the unpopular, pro-Catholic monarch James VII of Scotland, II of England, fled from London to France. In exile in Rome and Paris, adherents to the cause of restoration, who were known as Jacobites, worked to regain for the Stuarts the two thrones.

On the British Isles, Jacobite support came mainly from High Anglicans, Catholics, and Episcopalians and, by 1745, was centred in the Scottish Highlands. Since the great landowners of Perthshire were in the either Episcopalian or Catholic, it was an area to which Prince Edward Stuart looked for support. However, when the Prince landed on the west coast of Scotland to rally the Highland clans, with a few exceptions, he found the Clan Chiefs greatly reluctant to get involved. There had already been two unsuccessful campaigns, in the years 1715 and 1719, and it took all the legendary charm and powers of persuasion of the "Bonnie Prince", to convince these Chiefs that this time their efforts would bear fruit. The promise of substantial French assistance helped in no small part to win them over, and effected the gathering of the clans at Glenfinnan.

As it turned out, the pledged troops from France were very much fewer than the Prince had been led to expect, and the army which marched south was composed of highland and lowland Scots, Irish, English, when the Manchester Regiment joined in, and only a token number of French soldiers. In addition, although they advanced with very little resistance towards London, it soon became clear that the numbers of supporters expected to join the force south of the border were not doing so. When they arrived at Derby, only 100 miles from London, the dispirited and homesick army began to break up, at the same time as the House of Hanover belatedly awoke to the threat they posed. The king ordered his son, the Duke of Cumberland (Butcher Cumberland), to assemble his forces and march north. This Hanoverian army comprised regular English and lowland Scottish regiments, Dutch troops, and the Argyll Militia.

The culmination of the episode was played out on Drummossie Moor, Culloden in April 1745, when a badly commanded, ill prepared, wet and weary body of Jacobites, after marching through the night from Inverness, were ordered to charge the well-drilled and positioned, fresh Hanoverian army, many times greater in number. There followed slaughter on a grand scale, and after the battle, Cumberland commanded that his soldiers finish off the wounded that lay among the dead.

Those Jacobites who were able went into hiding, as did their Prince, who eventually escaped back to France. Others were rounded up and imprisoned in Inverness to await despatch south to their trials. Death from wounds, execution or transportation followed, and for the remaining Highland population, a way of life changed forever.

In 1715, and again in 1745 the aristocracy of Perthshire rallied in support of the House of Stuart. Much of this support was centred on the Murrays of Atholl and the Duke of Perth, and the majority of men from Perthshire who took part in the 1745 uprising were part of their two regiments. Many of the landed gentry hedged their bets, however, with one member paying lip service to the House of Hanover and the other supporting openly the House of Stuart.

The history of the Atholl Brigade is very typical of that of the Jacobite army generally, and shows clearly the difficulties encountered in both raising and retaining men. The popular belief that men flocked to the Prince's colours is, like so many popular ideas, unsupported by facts; and, from the time of the Prince's landing to the fall of the curtain at Culloden, the Jacobite army fluctuated in strength and composition to an extent which makes it impossible to estimate with accuracy what the numbers were at any particular time.

This fact is not in any part due to the absence of records as is clearly shown by the letters of Lord George Murray to his brother, the Jacobite Duke William, and to the subordinate leaders of the Atholl Brigade. Crushed with work and responsibility, that devoted and gallant servant of the Prince was compelled to write dozens of letters during the campaign, cajoling, entreating, and threatening, to raise the necessary men and to recover those who, having joined the colours, took the first opportunity to desert.

There was a widespread reluctance to join the 1745 uprising, and "the greatest force and violence was used" to limited effect. The men so pressed to join, deserted, and more effort had to be spent rounding them up again. For obvious reasons, desertions ceased during the expedition to England, but, on the return of the Prince's army to Scotland, they recommenced with devastating effects, causing Lord George Murray much anxiety. His brother, the Duke, meanwhile, did his best to raise more men, but spoke of "unspeakable difficulty with the refractory people in these parts", and he was apparently reluctant to "make the examples" suggested by the more masterful Lord George.

Lord James Drummond, the Duke of Perth, joined the Prince on 4 September 1745 at Perth, and then went home to raise support. He brought to Dunblane 150 men, including some Macgregors. In Edinburgh, on 18 September 1745 "a drum beat up for Volunteers, when a good many entered the Duke of Perth's regiment." At the battle of Prestonpans the regiment was reported to consist of 200 men, but by the time the march to England commenced, Patullo shows it had risen to 750, largely due to the addition of about 250 men raised by Sandilands and Charles Moir of Stonywood. An additional 300 were raised and brought by James Drummond, Master of Strathallan and a company of Robertson of Struan's.

References appear in Records of "The Red Coats of Perth's." This does not mean that they all wore red coats. The probable explanation is that many of the men were English soldiers taken at Prestonpans wearing their old English uniform.

The Duke of Perth's regiment was apparently responsible to a great extent, at least in the early stages of the campaign, for the safety of the Artillery of the army. Three companies were detailed for this duty.

The first mention of the Robertsons is when 140 tenants of Alexander Robertson of Struan in Rannoch joined the Prince in Glenalmond early in September 1745, and were incorporated in what became the Atholl Brigade. The old chief was actually present as a spectator at Prestonpans with his men, but then went home. On 25 September he wrote to his kinsman, Robertson of Woodshiel telling him and his men to join Keppoch's regiment, 'if they please'. Struan's Company was part of the Duke of Perth's regiment, but apparently most of Struan's men were ultimately merged in the Atholl Brigade.

Roy Stuart's regiment was sometimes called the Edinburgh regiment. He was a Jacobite agent who escaped from Inverness prison in 1736 and went abroad to France. He accompanied the Prince in Edinburgh and set about raising a regiment locally. The Stewarts of

Grantully, a Perthshire unit, joined Roy Stuart's regiment, but its strength had fallen to 200 at Culloden owing to a considerable number having been captured in the fall of the Carlisle garrison on 30 December 1745. For a time after Culloden Roy Stuart was in hiding, but eventually appears to have escaped to France along with the Prince.

Frances McDonnell
St Andrews, August 1998

REFERENCES

Archives

PRO Public Record Office, London

    CO   Colonial Office
    SP   State Papers
    T   Treasury

SRO Scottish Record Office, Edinburgh

    GD   Gifts and Deposits

Publications

CA   Chronicles of Atholl and Tullibardine,
          John, Duke of Atholl (Edinburgh, 1908)
F   *Fasti Ecclesiae Scoticanae*
          J Scott (Edinburgh, 1915)
GS   *Goteborg, Skottland och Vackre Prinsen*
          G. Behre (Goteborg, 1982)
MR   *The Muster Roll of Prince Charles Edward Stuart's*
          Army 1745-1746
          A. Livingstone (Aberdeen, 1984)
P   *Prisoners of the '45*
          B. Seton (Edinburgh, 1929)
SHS   *List of Persons Concerned in the Rebellion 1745-46*
          Earl of Roseberry (Edinburgh, 1890)

BLAIR CASTLE, 1736
FRONT ELEVATION

JACOBITES
OF PERTHSHIRE
1745

ABERNETHY, ALEXANDER, Captain, farmer, Tippertie, Duke of
Perth's Regiment, captured at siege of Carlisle, 30 Dec 1745, died
in Southward Prison, Aug 1746 *CA.3.131, P.1.186, MR.67*

ALEXANDER, CHARLES, Officer, Atholl Brigade, Factor to Struan,
accompanied Struan to Edinburgh *CA.3.299, MR.20*

ANDERSON, LAURENCE, servant to Lessendy, Pendreech, Lessendy,
Perthshire. "Joined the rebels as a volunteer some time before the
affair of Falkirk and went north." *SHS.8.196*

ANTON, ALEXANDER, shoemaker, Meigle, Perthshire. "Carried
arms, assisted Rattray of Dunoon in oppressing the country and
was at the battle of Culloden." Come home *SHS.8.198*

ARCHIBALD, JOHN, Sheriff Officer from Perth, imprisoned 10.2.1746
Perth, Edinburgh Jail 1.4.1746, released under General Pardon
1747, "On suspicion of treasonable practice" *P.2.16*

ATHOLL, WILLIAM, Duke of (1715, 1719) Lieutenant General, eldest
surviving son of 1st Duke, Col, 3rd Battalion, surrendered April and
died, Tower of London, July 1746 *CA.3.299*

BAIN, WILLIAM, labourer, Glenleighwin, Perthshire Duke of Perth's
Regiment, taken prisoner at Carlisle 30.12.1745, died? *MR.69*

BALFOUR, JOHN, Captain, Messenger at Arms, Perth, now lurking
SHS.8.42

BALLANTINE, JOHN, piper, Atholl Brigade, taken prisoner at Carlisle 30.12.1745, acquitted *MR.22*

BALNEVIS, JAMES, from Perth, age 58, imprisoned in Inverness, shipped on *James & Mary* to the Medway, servant to Drummond of Broich "Only on suspicion" SPD 86-55. Does not appear in the transportation lists, may have died *P.2.22*

BANNERMAN, JOHN, workman, Dunkeld, joined and assisted the rebels, whereabouts not known *CA.3.306, SHS.8.42*

BANNERMAN, JOHN, aged 20, 1st Battalion, Atholl Brigade, taken prisoner, died? *MR.22*

BARRIE, DAVID, cottar, Wester Kinnaird, Atholl Brigade, in south and in England (paid listing money) *CA.3.304, MR.22*

BARRIE, JAMES, in Torrievald, Atholl Brigade, in south and in England *CA.3.303, MR.22*

BARRIE, JOHN, cottar, Countlich, Atholl Brigade, (paid listing money) killed Culloden *CA.3.303, MR.22*

BAXTER, DAVID, weaver in Murray of Niviland's factory, Crieff, Perthshire, formerly of Cupar, Fife, Duke of Perth's Regiment, taken prisoner, transported 20 Mar 1747 from Tilbury, *P.2.30, MR.69*

BAXTER, DAVID, Servant to James Kinnie, Onthank, Forgan, Perthshire. "Carried arms with the rebels in Lord Otgilvie's Regiment, and was at the battles of Falkirk and Culloden." At home *SHS.8.198*

BAYNE, JAMES, Barber, Perth, acted as a quartermaster for the rebels, now lurking *SHS.8.42*

BEG, JAMES, cooper, Forgan, Perthshire. "Carried arms in Lord Ogilvie's regiment, and went with them to Perth." At home *SHS.8.198*

BINNIEVIS, JAMES, doctor, age 54, from Perthshire, shipped on *Margaret and Mary* to Tilbury. On suspicion – SPD 84-2. His name does not appear in the transportation lists, and he may have died at Tilbury *P.2.34*

BLAIR, GEORGE, from Alyth, Perthshire Horse, (Strathallan's Regiment) *MR.53*

BLAIR, THOMAS, Lieutenant Colonel, of Glasclune, 4th Battalion, Atholl Brigade, taken prisoner at Bergen, Norway, but escaped *CA.3.299, MR.18*

BOURNE, JOHN, Ogilvy's Regiment, 30.12.1745 in Carlisle Prison, and Chester Castle, from Huntingtower, Perth, cordwainer. Taken at capture of town SPD 81-293. There is no further reference to him *P.2.42*

BOWIE, JOHN, mason, Dunkeld, guarded Inver Ferry for the rebels, now at home *CA.3.306, SHS.8.42*

BOWIE, PAUL, Whitefield's, Atholl Brigade *MR.22*

BRESDIE, ROBERT, resident of Muthill, pressed out by Lord Drummond but returned, now at home. This may be the person whose birth is recorded in the Episcopal register of baptisms for Muthill, on 15 January 1724, as son of John Brady and Jean Ure *SHS.8.42, SHS.8.370*

BROMLEY, ANNE, Duke of Perth's Regiment, released 1747 *P.1.215*

BROWN, DAVID, merchant, Coupar Angus, Perthshire, carried arms, was at Inverury Skirmish and active in raising men, at home *SHS.8.198*

BROWN, DONALD, Whitefield's, Atholl Brigade *MR.22*

BROWN, JOHN, from Perth, 1.5.1746 imprisoned in Perth, discharged on bail 5.7.1746, "on suspicion" *P.2.54*

BROWNHILL, THOMAS, aged 22, (born 1725) labourer, Kinnaird, Inchture, Perthshire, 5'6" tall, fair complexion, slender, well made, Ogilvy's Regiment. Bore arms and went into England, taken at fall of Carlisle, imprisoned in Carlisle 30.12.1745, and Lincoln Castle, transported 5 May 1747 from Liverpool to Antigua, Leeward Islands on the *Veteran*, Master John Ricky, liberated by

French Privateer and landed on Martinique June 1747.
PRO.SP36.102,ff.120r-121v, P.2.52, P.2.53, SHS.8.200

BRUCE, JOHN, Whitefield's, Atholl Brigade *MR.22*

BUCHANAN, ALEXANDER, Captain, Duke of Perth's Regiment, son
of the Laird of Auchleishie, Auchleishie, parish of Callander,
13.6.1746 imprisoned in Perth, 8.8.1746 Cannongate prison,
9.8.1746 Carlisle prison, shipped on *Jane of Leith* to London,
acquitted, but by mistake transported 22 Apr 1747 from Liverpool
to Virginia on the *Johnson*, arrived Port Oxford, Maryland 5 Aug
1747 *SHS.8.54, P.2.58, MR.67, PRO.T1.328*. This was probably
Alexander Buchanan, son of the Laird of Auchleshie, Callander,
Perthshire, who "carried arms as a Captain in the rebell service,"
and was later shown as a prisoner in London. He was tried on 15
November, but was acquitted on account of being only 19 years of
age. His servant, John Buchanan, deponed that he had several
times deserted or tried to do so and that he was repeatedly forced
back. *Scots Mag 1746, 529*. Nevertheless his name appears in
the transportation list.

BUCHANAN, FRANCIS, of Arnprior, Lenny House, Callander,
Monteith, Perthshire, imprisoned in Lenny, Stirling Castle,
8.8.1746 Carlisle, executed 19.10.1746 in Carlisle. Arms
collected by Murray of Broughton before the Prince's landing were
lodged at the house of Francis Buchanan. He was arrested on
suspicion before Culloden. No charge was brought against him at
his trial except that an intercepted letter was stated to be in his
handwriting. In a statement just before his death he regretted that
he had not thrown in his lot openly with the Prince on his arrival
and drawn his sword. When he arrived at Carlisle he was put in
irons, and was told this was done by order of the Solicitor-General.
The latter, when approached in regard to the severity of this
treatment, said, "I have particular orders about him, for he must
suffer." An incident which occurred before his capture may
possibly have been connected with his case. Arnprior had been to
see Stewart of Glenbucky, and there had been some dispute about
the post of Major in the Perth Regiment to which Glenbucky
belonged. Arnprior brought Glenbucky home with him to Lenny
that night. The next morning he was found dead in bed with a
pistol in his hand. Arnprior said this had prejudiced him in his
trial, although he had no hand in his death. Writing to Philip
Webb on 9 Sept 1746, the Lord Justice Clerk said it would be of

"more consequence to His Majesty's Service...... to get rid of such a person than to convict 99 of the lowest rank." *P.2.58*

BUCHANAN, JOHN, Auchterarder, age 22, Duke of Perth's Regiment, Buchanan's company, carried arms as a volunteer in the rebel army, prisoner at Auchterarder 7.5.1746; Stirling Castle, and Carlisle prisons, Servant to Capt Alexander Buchanan, transported 24 Feb 1747 from Liverpool to Virginia on the *Gildart*, arrived at Port North Potomac, Maryland 5 Aug 1747 *SHS.8.42, P.2.60, MR.69, PRO.T1.328, P.2.60*

BUCHANAN, JOHN, brewer, Kilmahog parish of Callander, joined the rebels and went with them to Crieff, now at home *SHS.8.54*

BUCHANAN, PATRICK, brewer, Kilmahog, parish of Callander, joined rebels and went with them to Crieff, acquitted 12.9.1746, brother of Francis Buchanan of Arnprior, he was tried at Carlisle and acquitted *SHS.8.54, P.2.60*

BUCHANAN, ROBERT, Captain, son of Baillie Buchanan in Boghastle, Boghastle, Callander, at battle of Culloden, killed there *SHS.8.54*

BULLEN, PATRICK, Perthshire, Robertson's of Woodsheal's Regiment, Atholl Brigade, imprisoned 10.8.1746 in Canongate, released under General Pardon, 1747 *P.2.62*

BURT, JAMES, shoemaker, Perth, Perthshire Horse, (Strathallan's Regiment) seen in arms with the rebels, now lurking *SHS.8.42, MR.55*

BUTLER, PATRICK, Perthshire, Tullibardine's (ie Atholl's) Regiment, 24.6.1746 imprisoned in Perth, 9.8.1746 Carlisle prison, acquitted 19.9.1746 *P.2.66*

BUTTAR, PATRICK, in Dunfalandy, at Culloden *CA.3.305*

BUTTAR, THOMAS, in Dunfalandy, Atholl Brigade, at Culloden (paid listing money) *CA.3.305, MR.22*

BUTTER, ALEXANDER, Officer, at Faskally Atholl Brigade, *CA.3.299, MR.20*

BUTTER, DAVID, in Drum, servant , (paid listing money), Atholl Brigade, killed, at Culloden *CA.3.303, MR.22*

BUTTER, DONALD, in Ballintylar, at Culloden *CA.3.303, MR.22*

BUTTER, PATRICK, younger of Kinhard, Officer, Atholl Brigade, in south and in England, surrendered, tried, acquitted *CA.3.299 CA.3.304, MR.20*

BUTTER, PETER, portioner of Easter Dunfallandie, Officer, Atholl Brigade, with Struan's men *CA.3.299, CA.3.307, MR.20*

CADDELL, ROBERT, Doune, Perthshire, 24.4.1746 in Stirling prison, released under General Pardon, 1747, Gunsmith "In the rebellion", *P.2.66*

CAMERON, ALEXANDER, in Pitlochry, Atholl Brigade, in south and in England (paid listing money) (possibly transported 22 Apr 1747 from Liverpool to Virginia on *Johnson*, arriving Port Oxford, Maryland, 5 Aug 1747 *PRO.T1.328, CA.3.304*

CAMERON, ALEXANDER, from Perth, Struan Robertson's Regiment, Atholl Brigade, 4.11.1745 imprisoned in Pentland Hills and Edinburgh Castle, 15.1.1746 in Edinburgh Jail, released under General Pardon, 1747, "A common highlander". This man was caught when trying to desert, along with three other Camerons *P.2.72, MR.22*

CAMERON, ALLAN, Perthshire, Duke of Perth's Regiment, 12.5.1746 in Perth Prison, died 25.7.1746 *P.2.72, MR.70, P.1.186*

CAMERON, DUNCAN, Rev, Episcopal minister, Fortingall, Chaplain, Lochiel's Regiment *CA.3.299*

CAMERON, JAMES, Perth, 15.5.1746 imprisoned in Perth, discharged on bail 8.7.1746, "on suspicion" *P.2.82*

CAMPBELL, ...?, Ensign, of Tomnagrew, Grandtully's man in Roy Stewart's Regiment, killed, Culloden *CA.3.299*

CAMPBELL, ...?, Captain, son of the Laird of Glenlyon, parish of Fortingall, now lurking *SHS.8.42*

CAMPBELL, ARCHIBALD (ROY), Captain, youngest son of John Campbell of Glenlyon, Atholl Brigade, afterwards Lieutenant in Fraser's Highlanders, pardoned, severely wounded at Quebec, 1760 *CA.3.299, MR.18*

CAMPBELL, BARBRA, aged 19, spinner, Perthshire, red hair, clever, imprisoned in Carlisle and Chester Castle, transported 5 May 1747 from Liverpool to the Leeward Islands on the *Veteran*, liberated by a French Privateer and landed on Martinique June 1747 *PRO.SP36.102,ff.120r-121v, P.2.90.*

CAMPBELL, DANIEL, aged 19, 2nd Battalion, Atholl Brigade, transported 31 Mar 1747 from Tilbury to Barbados, in *Frere*, *P.2.90, MR.22*

CAMPBELL, DONALD, in Ballnamuir, servant, in south and in England *CA.3.303*

CAMPBELL, DONALD, aged 20, herd to Dalchosnie, Lord G Murray's Regiment, taken south in May 1746 on board *Jane* of Leith, transported 31 Mar 1747 from Tilbury to Jamaica on *St George* or *Carteret CA.3.316, MR.22, PRO.CO137.58*

CAMPBELL, DONALD, from Perth, aged 28, Lord George Murray's Regiment, 2nd Battalion, Atholl Brigade, herded cattle to Alexander McDonald of Dalchosnie, imprisoned in Inverness, shipped on *Liberty and Property* June 1746 to Medway, Tilbury, transported 31 Mar 1747 *P.2.90, MR.22*

CAMPBELL, DUNCAN, brother to Dunnevis, Officer *CA.3.299*

CAMPBELL, DUNCAN, in Dunchastle, at Culloden (paid listing money) *CA.3.304*

CAMPBELL, DUNCAN, aged 17, apprentice tailor, Breadalbane, South Uist, 2nd Battalion, Atholl Brigade, Lord George Murray's Regiment taken south in May 1746 on board *Jane of Leith*, turned King's Evidence, discharged *CA.3.316, MR.22*

CAMPBELL, DUNCAN, brother of the Laird of Dunneves, parish of Fortingall, Officer, Atholl Brigade, now lurking *SHS.8.42, MR.20*

CAMPBELL, DUNCAN, Drumcastle, Atholl Brigade *MR.22*

CAMPBELL, DUNCAN, aged 19, from Perth, Lord George Murray's Regiment, 2nd Battalion, Atholl Brigade, imprisoned in Inverness June 1746, shipped on *Alexander and James* to Tilbury, no further reference to his disposal *P.2.92, MR.22*

CAMPBELL, FINLAY, in Ballachandie, servant (paid listing money), at Culloden *CA.3.304, MR.23*

CAMPBELL, (or McGREGOR) JAMES, from Crieff, Perthshire, Piper, Glengyle's Regiment, imprisoned in Carlisle, pleaded guilty at his trial on 9 Sept 1746 and was sentenced to death. He was reprieved, and tried to escape the night before he was transported. Transported on *Elizabeth*, Master Daniel Cole, from Liverpool to Jamaica 6.2.1748, but landed in Antigua 21.3.1748 *P.2.94, PRO.T53.44*

CAMPBELL, JOHN, Atholl, 3rd Battalion, Atholl Brigade, taken prisoner, discharged *MR.23*

CAMPBELL, JOHN, of Kinloch, Lieutenant, Grandtully's man in Roy Stewart's Regiment, killed, Culloden *CA.3.298, CA.3.299*

CAMPBELL, JOHN, (1715) of Glenlyon, too old for service but sent his men *CA.3.299*

CAMPBELL, JOHN, born 1732, servant from Rannoch, transported 5 May 1747 from Liverpool to the Leeward Islands on *Veteran*, liberated by a French Privateer and landed on Martinique June 1747 *P.6.96, MR.151, PRO.SP36.102*

CAMPBELL, JOHN, Captain in Roy Stuart's Regiment, of Kinloch, Milton of Strathbran, Little Dunkeld parish, prisoner in Inverness June 1746, shipped south on *Thane of Fife*, *SHS.8.42, P.2.94*

CAMPBELL, JOHN, Perthshire, Tullibardine's Regiment, wounded 22.9.1745, imprisoned in Edinburgh Royal Infirmary, 5.5.1746 in the Canongate prison, released under General Pardon, 1747, gunshot wound at Musselburgh "wants left leg" *P.2.96, MR.23*

CAMPBELL, MARTHA, Duke of Perth's Regiment, released 1747, *P.1.216*

CAMPBELL, MUNGO, Officer, Milnrogie, Glenalmond, Atholl Brigade, *CA.3.299, MR.20*

CAMPBELL, MUNGO, Ensign in Glengyle's Regiment, late soldier in Lord John Murray's Regiment, Crieff, imprisoned in Perth 23.3.1747, discharged on bail 11.7.1747 *SHS.8.42, P.2.98, MR.167*

CAMPBELL, PETER, from Annandale, Duke of Perth's Regiment, taken at Carlisle, pardoned on enlistment *MR.70*

CAMPBELL, WILLIAM, aged 21, born 1726, weaver, Grandtully, Perthshire, 5'6" tall, fair, thin, writes well, healthy, captured at the siege of Carlisle 30 Dec 1745, imprisoned in Carlisle and Lancaster Castle, transported 5 May 1747 from Liverpool to Antigua, Leeward Islands on *Veteran*, liberated by a French Privateer and landed on Martinique June 1747, *P.2.98, MR.206, PRO.SP36.102,ff.120r-121v, CA.3.132*

CANDO, JOHN, weaver, Kincairnie, Caputh, Perthshire, carried arms, whereabouts not known *SHS.8.200*

CARMICHAEL, DAVID, of Balmedie. This family is said to have descended from Robert, second son of Sir John de Carmichael of that ilk, who fought at the battle of Beauge in 1421. David, mentioned in the List, was probably not the Laird of Balmedie, who at that time is understood to have been Thomas Carmichael, who died in 1746, leaving an only son James, afterwareds distinguished as a physician.

CARMICHAEL, JOHN, of Baiglie, in the same parish as David Carmichael, whose representative is now an officer in the French navy, was also out in the '45. The person named on the same page of the List as collector of the stent may well have been the laird of Baiglie; he was related to the Balmedie family *SHS.8.370*

CARMICHAEL, JOHN, Collector of the Stent in Perth, Woodend, Kinnoull, joined the rebels and went north with them, whereabouts not known *SHS.8.42*

CARROLL, MARY, from Perth, aged 19, captured at fall of Carlisle, imprisoned in Carlisle and Lancaster Castle, "a clever lass" no further reference to her *P.2.102*

CATHEL, AGNES, from Monteith, Roy Stuart's Regiment, imprisoned
3.12.1745 in Carlisle with a child of 3, taken after the capture of
Carlisle, released *P.2.104*

CAW, LODOVICK, surgeon, Crieff, acted as surgeon to Duke of Perth's
Regiment and went with the rebels, whereabouts not known
SHS.8.42, MR.68

CELLARS, CHARLES, from Perth, Roy Stuart's (Edinburgh) Regiment,
imprisoned 29.11.1746 Perth, escaped 7.3.1747 *P.2.106, MR.206*

CHALMERS, FRANCIS, servant to Lord George Murray, 2nd Battalion,
Atholl Brigade, surrendered, turned King's Evidence, released
MR.23

CHALMERS, (or CAMERON) PETER, from Dunkeld, imprisoned
22.7.1746 captured on board a ship *Adam Hendry* in Leith Roads,
imprisoned 22.7.1746 Leith, 18.8.1746 Canongate, escaped
25.12.1746, vintner's servant, "on suspicion" *P.2.108*

CHALMERS, THOMAS, from Whitside, Alyth, Perthshire, son of
William Chalmers, Ogilvy's Regiment, 30.12.1745 Carlisle prison,
Chester Castle and London, discharged. Son of William
Chalmers. Taken at Carlisle on the surrender of the town to
Cumberland on 30.12.1745. He was sent to London, where he
gave evidence against other prisoners, and his name appears as in
the custody of Carrington the messenger in June 1747 *P.2.108,
SHS.8.204*

CHAMBERS, JOHN, aged 21, born 1726, labourer, Perthshire, 5'9" tall,
dark hair, well made, imprisoned in Carlisle and Lancaster Castle,
transported 5 May 1747 from Liverpool to Antigua, Leeward
Islands on *Veteran*, liberated by French Privateer, and landed on
Martinique June 1747, *P.2.108, PRO.SP36.102,ff.120r-121v,
P.2.110*

CHAPE (or CHEAP), MATTHEW, Private, sadler with Beaglie,
Perthshire Horse, (Strathallan's Regiment), carried arms, prisoner
in Perth 1.5.1746, discharged on bail 16.3.1747, pardoned
SHS.8.42, P.2.110, MR.54

CLARK, HENRY, Perthshire, McIntosh's Regiment, imprisoned
27.2.1746 in Perth, then Edinburgh, and 8.8.1746 in Carlisle, died

in prison November 1746. Gentleman, an Officer. It is said he had carried arms and had robbed Mr Scot's house. He pleaded guilty when arraigned and was sentenced to death 22 Aug 1746, but he died in prison *P.2.116*

CLARK, JOHN, mason, Dunkeld, took prisoner the excise officer and beat him, surrendered himself, released under General pardon, 1747 *CA.3.306, SHS.8.44, P.2.116*

CLARK, WILLIAM, farmer, Callendar Duke of Perth's Regiment, "on suspicion" imprisoned 23.3.1746 in Stirling and London, turned King's Evidence, discharged 29.4.1746 *P.2.118, MR.70*

COCHRANE, JOHN, Perthshire, imprisoned 24.6.1746 "on suspicion", Perth, discharged on bail 3.7.1746 *P.2.120*

COCHRANE, WILLIAM, senior, Captain, Jackstown, Strathord, Auchtergaven, Factor to Lord Nairne, 1st Battalion Atholl Brigade, was active in persuading the tenants to rise in Rebellion, at home *CA.3.299, CA.3.306, MR.18, SHS.8.200*

COCHRANE, WILLIAM, jnr, wright, Jackstown, Auchtergaven, Perthshire, 1st Battalion, Atholl Brigade, was servant to Lord Nairn, appeared early in arms, whereabouts not known *MR.23, SHS.8.200*

COLVILLE, GEORGE, Hon., brother to Lord Colville, physician in Dundee, surgeon to Duke William *CA.3.299*

COMRIE, DUNCAN, resident of Woodend of Mevie, parish of Comrie, carried arms but pressed thereto, whereabouts not known *SHS.8.44*

COMRIE, JOHN, Captain, Duke of Perth's Regiment, captured and died at siege of Carlisle, 30 Dec 1747, *CA.3.131*

CONACHER, CHARLES, younger, fisher in Logierait, at Culloden *CA.3.303, MR.23*

CRANE, PETER, age 19, hardwareman from Perthshire, imprisoned in Carlisle and Lancaster Castle, transported 21.2.1747 *P.2.132*

CREIGHTON, JOHN, labourer from Cablen, Perthshire, Royal Stuart's Regiment, 30.12.1745 imprisoned in Carlisle and Chester Castle, transported 21.2.1747 from Liverpool to Virginia on *Gildart*, landed at Port North Potomac, Maryland 5 Aug 1747 *P.2.134, MR.97, PRO.T1.328*

CRICHTON, JOHN, gardener, Crummond, Duke of Perth's Regiment, taken prisoner, pardoned *MR.70*

CROCKAT, WILLIAM, son to Dr Crockat, Coupar Angus, Perthshire, carried arms and was at Culloden etc, and was active in raising men and money, lurking *SHS.8.204*

CROOK, ALEXANDER, senior, Coupar Angus, Perthshire, Surgeon Major Surgeon, Atholl Brigade, forced out, was in England, has charge of the sick soldiers at Coupar Angus, deserted, keeps his own house at General Husk's desire *CA.3.299, MR.18, SHS.8.204*

CROOK, ALEXANDER, son of Surgeon-Major Crook of Coupar Angus, his father's servant, Atholl Brigade, deserted, was in arms for the rebels, he and his father returned home 5 February 1746 *CA.3.299, MR.23, SHS.8.204*

CUMING, ALEXANDER, Captain, Duke of Perth's Regiment, sen, farmer, Meikle Crichie, brother to Kininmonth, Catholic, Miln of Drummond, Muthill, volunteer, taken prisoner, discharged *SHS.8.44, MR.67*

DEWAR, THOMAS, Perthshire, imprisoned 4.7.1746 in Perth, discharged 30.7.1746 "on suspicion"*P.2.152*

DICK, JOHN, butcher from Coupar Angus, imprisoned 4.5.1746 in Prestonpans and 6.5.1746 Canongate "on suspicion" "Witnesses say that they saw the prisoner killing cows and sheep for the use of the rebels at Bannockburn." "He joined the rebels on their march for England." *P.2.154*

DICK, WILLIAM, servant to Kincairney, Caputh (Mungo Murray, younger of Kincairney), 3rd Battalion, Atholl Brigade, carried arms during the whole uprising as a volunteer *CA.3.306, MR.23, SHS.8.206*

DICKSON, JAMES, in Easter Dalguise, in south and in England, Atholl Brigade *CA.3.305, MR.23*

DONALDSON, ANDREW, Dunkeld, merchant *CA.3.307*

DOUGAL, ANDREW, Stanley, Auchtergavin, 1st Battalion, Atholl Brigade *MR.23*

DOUGLAS, ROBERT, in Craigbea, tenant, Atholl Brigade, at Culloden *CA.3.304, MR.23*

DOUNY, ALEXANDER, servant, Mireside, Coupar Angus, Perthshire, carried arms, and was at the battle of Culloden, at home *SHS.8.206*

DOW, ALLAN, labourer, Glenfinglas parish of Callander, was at the Battle of Culloden, and killed there *SHS.8.54*

DOW, JOHN, born 1717 from Auchtergavin, Stanley, servant to Lord Nairne, 1st Battalion, Atholl Brigade, carried arms during the whole rebellion as a volunteer, transported 24 Feb 1747 from Liverpool to Virginia on *Gildart*, landed Port North Potomac, Maryland 5 Aug 1747, *P.2.162, MR.23, PRO.T1.328, CA.3.306, SHS.8.206*

DOW, WILLIAM, Lt, Duke of Perth's Regiment, Auchinshelloch, Comrie, Perthshire, imprisoned 3.1.1747 in Perth, discharged 13.7.1747 "acted as overseer under the French Engineer; said to be pressed" *SHS.8.44, P.2.162*

DRUMMOND – see McGregor

DRUMMOND, ?, factor to Drummond of Perth, "was very active in seducing gentlemen from their duty and loyalty to his Majesty," now at home *SHS.8.54*

DRUMMOND, ANDREW DOUGAL, servant to Lord Nairn at Logiealmond, Muneddie, Perthshire, carried arms during the whole uprising as a volunteer, whereabouts not known *SHS.8.206*

DRUMMOND, GAVIN, brewer, Auchterarder, was active in forcing people into the rebellion by the Duke of Perth's order, whereabouts not known *SHS.8.44*

DRUMMOND, GEORGE, Captain, Duke of Perth's Regiment, baker, Drummawhance, Perth, carried arms as a volunteer, imprisoned 7.2.1746 Perth and in Edinburgh, died 18.7.1746 in Edinburgh *SHS.8.44, P.2.162, MR.67, P.1.186*

DRUMMOND, GILBERT, born 1714, from Caputh, Meikleour, Perthshire, Duke of Perth's Regiment, servant to Mrs Robert Mercer of Aldie, and Colonel Mercer, imprisoned 25.2.1746 in Canongate and 8.8.1746 in Carlisle, "said to have carried arms as a volunteer during the whole rebellion" transported from Liverpool, died at sea 7 Jun 1747, *P.2.162, PRO.T1.328, CA.3.306, P.2.162, MR.23, P.1.186, SHS.8.206*

DRUMMOND, JAMES, tenant, Garthlees, carried arms as a volunteer, prisoner in Edinburgh *SHS.8.44*

DRUMMOND, JAMES, Comrie, carried arms, said to be pressed, now at home *SHS.8.44*

DRUMMOND, (Duke of Perth) JAMES, Lieutenant General, Drummond, Muthill, very active, died escaping to France. Son of James, Duke of Perth, by his wife, Lady Jean Gordon, daughter of George, Duke of Gordon. James, the father, was in the rebellion of 1715, and, escaping to France, resided there until 1730, when he died at Paris. Although attainted, his son succeeded to the estates under a disposition executed by him in 1713. On the arrival of the Pretender at Perth in September 1745, he was joined by the Duke of Perth, who was appointed Lieutenant-General in conjunction with Lord George Murray. He and his following were conspicuous throughout the campaign. After the defeat at Culloden he embarked for France, but died at sea on 11 May 1746, at the age of 33. His younger and only brother, Lord John Drummond, was his heir: he was an officer in the service of the French King, for whom he raised the regiment then called the Royal Scots, of which he was colonel. In November 1745 he arrived at Montrose with some French auxiliaries and a train of artillery for the service of the Chevalier, whom he joined just before the battle of Falkirk. After Culloden he returned to France, and died in 1747. *SHS.8.44, SHS.8.371*

DRUMMOND, JAMES, Cochquhillie, Muthill, volunteer, whereabouts not known *SHS.8.44*

DRUMMOND, JAMES, in Edradour, in south and in England, (paid listing money) *CA.3.304, MR.23*

DRUMMOND, JAMES, Duke of Perth's Regiment, aged 21 from Perth, imprisoned Inverness June 1746, shipped on *Wallsgrave* to Tilbury

Fort, released 20.6.1747, servant to John Drummond, Mailimore. He gave evidence against Lieutenant Charles Oliphant. Was for some months in the house of Dick the messenger *P.2.164*

DRUMMOND, JAMES, Lieutenant Colonel, Master of Strathallan, escaped *MR.67, SHS.8.372*

DRUMMOND, JOHN, Messenger at Arms, from Perth, imprisoned in Perth. Acted as overseer under the French Engineer, said to be pressed. The "French Engineer" was M. Mirabelle de Gordon, who was very incompetent in carrying out the siege operations against Stirling Castle *SHS.8.44, P.2.164*

DRUMMOND, JOHN, Captain, Duke of Perth's Regiment, Millinow, Comrie, now lurking *SHS.8.44, MR.67*

DRUMMOND, JOHN, Drummond, Muthill, volunteer, now at home *SHS.8.44, MR.71*

DRUMMOND, JOHN, aged 33, Drummond, Muthill, Perthshire, Valet to Duke of Perth, Duke of Perth's Regiment, volunteer, imprisoned Inverness June 1746, shipped on *Wallsgrave* Aug 1746 to Tilbury Fort, discharged. "Waited on the Duke for over a year." This may have been the John Drummond who turned King's Evidence against some of his fellow prisoners, eg Adam Hay of Asslid *P.2.164, SHS.8.44, MR71*

DRUMMOND, (or McGREGOR) JOHN, ? Captain in Glengyle's Regiment, from Balnacuik, Balquhidder, imprisoned 10.8.1746 in Canongate and Carlisle, transported 1747. This was perhaps nephew of William Drummond (or McGregor) of Balhaldie. He was 'lurking' for some time after Culloden *P.2.164, MR.167*

DRUMMOND, JOHN, of Dalpowie, Officer, Atholl Brigade, *CA.3.300, MR.20*

DRUMMOND, PETER (or PATRICK), Ensign, Bellnae, Comrie, imprisoned 23.3.1746 in Stirling, discharged 19.5.1746. "On suspicion". It is doubtful whether he was the Ensign or the Volunteer in the Prince's Army, both of whom came from Comrie. *SHS.8.44, P.2.166, MR.68, MR.71*

DRUMMOND, THOMAS, of Logie Almond, Muneddie, Perthshire, imprisoned May 1746 in Stirling Castle, released under General Pardon, 1747. He gave shelter to the Duke of Perth when Sir Patrick Murray of Ochtertyoungere had actually tried to capture the Duke in his own house. The Duke took refuge in Logie Almond. "Subsisted himself" (in prison) "Suspected of treason" *P.1.166*

DRUMMOND, WILLIAM, Captain, Duke of Perth's Regiment, of Callender, parish of Monzie, brother of William Drummond, 4th Viscount of Strathallan (1690-1746), son of Sir John Drummond of Machany, Perthshire and Margaret, daughter of Sir William Stewart of Innernytie. Escaped to Sweden *SHS.8.44, MR.67, GS.112*

DRUMMOND, WILLIAM, The Lord Strathallan, fourth Viscount: was in the rebellion in 1715, and taken prisoner at Sheriffmuir, but was subjected to forfeiture for that occasion. He received a leading command in the army of the Chevalier in 1745, and fell at Culloden. His wife was Lady Margaret Murray, daughter of the Baroness Nairne, by whom he had seven sons and six daughters. His eldest son, James, having also taken part in the rebellion was attainted, and died abroad in 1765. The attainder was taken off in 1824 *SHS.8.372*

DRYSDALE, JAMES, Muthill, Perthshire, Duke of Perth's Regiment, pressed into service, now at home *SHS.8.44, MR.71*

DUFF, ALEXANDER, in Dalmarnock, cottar, Atholl Brigade, in south and in England, killed *CA.3.303, MR.23*

DUFF, CHARLES, Dunkeld, labourer *CA.3.307*

DUFF, DANIEL, born 1721, labourer, Perthshire, 5'8" tall, cross made, strong, healthy, Roy Stuart's Regiment, taken after siege of Carlisle and imprisoned 30.12.1745 in Carlisle and in Lincoln Castle, transported 8 May 1747 from Liverpool to Leeward Islands on Veteran, liberated by a French Privateer and landed on Martinique Jun 1747, *P.2.168, MR.206, PRO.SP36.102,ff.120r-121v, P.2.168*

DUFF, DANIEL, soldier in Roy Stewart's Regiment, captured at the siege of Carlisle 30 Dec 1745 *CA.3.132*

DUFF, DANIEL, Atholl, Perthshire, soldier in Lord Ogilvie's Regiment, captured at the siege of Carlisle 30 Dec 1745, transported 21 Apr 1747 from London to Barbados on *Frere, P.2.168, CA.3.132*

DUFF, JAMES, in Dalmarnock, Strathbraan, Atholl Brigade, at Culloden, transported 1747 from Liverpool, *P.2.168, MR.206, CA.3.303, MR.23*

DUFF, JAMES, from Strathbraan or Grandtully, soldier in Roy Stewart's Regiment, captured and imprisoned after the siege of Carlisle 30 Dec 1745, transported *CA.3.132, P.2.168*

DUFF, JOHN, in Glenalbert, Atholl Brigade, in south and in England *CA.3.304, MR.23*

DUFF, JOHN, in Ballinluig, Atholl Brigade, in south and in England (paid listing money) *CA.3.304, MR.23*

DUFF, JOHN, labourer in Kirkton, Perthshire, soldier in Roy Stewart's (Edinburgh) Regiment, captured at the siege of Carlisle 30 Dec 1745, imprisoned in Carlisle and Chester Castle, transported 22 Apr 1747, from Liverpool to Virginia on *Johnson*, landed at Port Oxford, Maryland, 5 Aug 1747, *P.2.168, MR.206, PRO.T1.328, CA.3.132, P.2.168*

DUFF, ROBERT, servant to Wester Kinnaird, Atholl Brigade, in south and in England (paid listing money) *CA.3.304, MR.23*

DUFF, WILLIAM, servant to Ballnacree, Atholl Brigade, at Culloden (paid listing money) *CA.3.304, MR.23*

DUK, JOHN, butcher from Coupar Angus, imprisoned 4.5.1746 Prestonpans; 6.5.1746 Edinburgh Jail, released under General Pardon, 1747. "On suspicion" *P.2.168*

DUNCAN, JEAN, Duke of Perth's Regiment, released 1747 *P.1.216*

DUNCAN, JOHN, from Perthshire, Ogilvy's Regiment, imprisoned 30.4.1746; 8.8.1746 Canongate; Aug 1746 Carlisle; transported "servant to Captain John Kinloch" *P.2.170*

FARQUHAR, WILLIAM, tailor, Alyth, Perthshire, carried arms in Lord Ogilvie's 2nd Battalion, lurking near home *SHS.8.212*

FARQUHAR, PATRICK, servant, Alyth, Perthshire, bore arms at Inverury skirmish, lurking *SHS.8.212*

FARQUHARSON, ALEXANDER, in Ballaghulan, Atholl Brigade, in south and in England (paid listing money) (possibly transported 31 Mar 1747 from London to Barbados on Frere, *P.2.182, MR.202, CA.3.304, MR.23*

FARQUHARSON, ANDREW, from Stratherrol, imprisoned 6.7.1746 Stratherrol, 6.7.1746 Dundee, discharged 16.3.1747 "forced out by the rebels" *P.1.182*

FARQUHARSON, CHARLES, The Rev, from Braemar, imprisoned Inverness, Tilbury, Southwark, in custody of Dick the Messenger, released on condition of departing the Kingdom and not returning, May 1747. "Jesuit Priest. Was a witness to his brother, John, at Strathglass. He left Scotland in 1729, studied at Madrid and Douai, and in obedience to the order of his superior, Francisco Ritz, General of the Jesuits, delivered to him on 26 July last, he returned to Scotland and, being appointed to no certain place, he went to his brother, said John" *P.2.182*

FARQUHARSON, DONALD, aged 48, farmer, Balquhidder, Perthshire, Duke of Perth's Regiment, imprisoned Inverness June 1746, shipped on *Liberty and Property* to Medway, transported 31.3.1747 from London to Barbados on *Frere P.2.182, MR.71*

FARQUHARSON, JOHN, of Strathglass, The Rev, S.J. from Braemar, imprisoned Inverness Sept 1746, shipped on *Pamela* to Tilbury, 9 Apr 1747 Southward, in custody of Dick the Messenger, released on condition of leaving the Kingdom and not returning, May 1747. "Jesuit. He left Scotland 1714, studied at Douai and other colleges in Flanders, and in 1729 returned to Scotland by order of the then General of the Jesuits and lived ever since in Strathglass" *P.2.184*

FARQUHARSON, ROBERT, aged 21, from Perth, servant to Mr Robertson in Balnacraig, Lord George Murray's Regiment, 2nd Battalion, Atholl Brigade, imprisoned in Inverness; taken south on *Wallsgrave* Tilbury Fort in May 1746 on board *Jane of Leith*, died *CA.3.316, P.2.186, MR.23*

FERGUSON (or FERGUS), ADAM, in Edradour, Atholl Brigade, in south and in England (paid listing money) *CA.3.304*

FERGUSON, ALEXANDER, Whitefield's, Atholl Brigade *MR.23*

FERGUSON, ARCHIBALD, brother of Thomas Ferguson of Balyoukan, Officer, Atholl Brigade, *CA.3.300, MR.20*

FERGUSON, DANIEL, aged 48, from Perth, Duke of Perth's Regiment, imprisoned in Inverness, shipped on *Margaret and Mary* to Tilbury. There is no further reference to him, he may have died *P.2.186, MR.71*

FERGUSON, DUNCAN, aged 34, farmer from Perthshire, Duke of Perth's Regiment, imprisoned 13.6.1746 in Perth; 10.8.1746 Canongate, Carlisle, Lancaster Castle, transported 22 Apr 1747 from Liverpool to Virginia on *Johnson* landed at Port Oxford, Maryland 5 Aug 1747 *P.2.188, MR.71, PRO.T1.328*

FERGUSON, FERGUS, Glenelbert, fisher *CA.3.307*

FERGUSON, HUGH, Stanley, servant to Lord Nairne, 1st Battalion, Atholl Brigade, died Perth 15.4.1747 *CA.3.306, MR.23, P.1.186*

FERGUSON, HUGH, from Perthshire, Duke of Perth's Regiment, imprisoned 22.12.1746 Perth, died 15.4.1747 *P.2.188, MR.71*

FERGUSON, JAMES, younger of Baledmund, Officer, Atholl Brigade, taken prisoner, tried, acquitted *CA.3.300, MR.20*

FERGUSON, JAMES, in Pitcastle, in south and in England *CA.3.303*

FERGUSON, JAMES, of Dumfallandy, imprisoned 24.6.1746 Perth, 10.8.1746 Canongate, Carlisle, tried, acquitted 9.9.1746, *CA.3.300, CA.3.307, P.2.188*

FERGUSON, JAMES, son to John Ferguson in Dunfalandy, Atholl Brigade, killed at Culloden (paid listing money) *CA.3.305, MR.23*

FERGUSON, JOHN, aged 20, Perthshire, Lord George Murray's Regiment, 2nd Battalion, Atholl Brigade, imprisoned in Inverness, shipped on *Wallsgrave* to Tilbury. No further reference to him *P.2.188, MR.23*

FERGUSON, MURDOCH, Dunblane, imprisoned 2.2.1746 Dunblane; 7.2.1746 Stirling Castle; 13.2.1746 Leith, discharged 20.6.1746. "A common carrier" *P.2.188*

FERGUSON, PATRICK, aged 80?, labourer from Perthshire, Duke of Perth's Regiment, imprisoned 30.12.1745 Carlisle; Lancaster Castle. Taken at capture of Carlisle, "old and gray". His age and the fact that he was not transported suggest that he died *P.2.190, MR.71*

FERGUSON, PETER (or PATRICK), from Callander, tenant to Robertson of Struan. "Suspicion of being in rebellion". Robertson's Regiment, Atholl Brigade, imprisoned 14.11.1745 Stirling Castle, 23.3.1746 Stirling, discharged 29.4.1746 *P.2.190, MR.23*

FERGUSON, PAUL, Whitefield's, Atholl Brigade *MR.23*

FERGUSON, ROBERT, Whitefield's, Atholl Brigade *MR.23*

FERGUSON, ROBERT, in Middlehaugh (a young man), Atholl Brigade, in south and in England *CA.3.304, MR.23*

FERGUSON, THOMAS, Captain, younger of Balyoukan, Atholl Brigade, wounded, at Culloden *CA.3.298, CA.3.300, CA.3.304, CA.3.308, MR.18*

FERGUSON, WILLIAM, from Moevie, Comrie, Perthshire, Duke of Perth's Regiment, imprisoned near Nairn House; 11.2.1746 Perth, 30.3.1746 Edinburgh, 8.8.1746 Carlisle. Tenant of Duke of Perth in Moevie. Does not appear in the transportation lists, may have died in prison *P.2.190, MR.71*

FISHER, DANIEL, from Perthshire, Duke of Perth's Regiment, imprisoned 30.12.1745 in Carlisle. Taken at capture of Carlisle. His name does not appear again, and he may have died *P.2.192*

FLEMING, DAVID, from Perth, imprisoned 10.2.1746 Perth; 1.4.1746 Edinburgh Jail, discharged. Sheriff Officer, Perth. "Suspicion of treasonable practices." "Ran errands for the rebels and went at their desire to warn in carts and horses from the country to carry their baggage" *P.2.198*

FLEMING, ROBERT, in Edradour, Atholl Brigade, in south and in England, (paid listing money) *CA.3.304, MR.23*

FOGO, JOHN, farmer, Balmacolly, Auchtergaven, Perthshire, ground officer to Lord Nairne, active but not out. "Was in the Council house of Perth with the rebels on the anniversary of his Majesty's birthday but accidentally: he being Lord Nairn's factor came into Perth that night about some private business of his Master's, at which instant a tumult happening 'twixt the Town's People and the Rebels he fled into the Council house fearing violence from the former on his said Master's account whom they knew to be in the Rebellion. He never carried arms nor had any station in the rebel army, this by certain intelligence." *CA.3.306, SHS.8.212*

FORBES, DONALD, in Moulin, Atholl Brigade, in south and in England *CA.3.304, MR.23*

FORBES, GEORGE, Factor to Lady Strathmore, Castle Lyon, Forgan, Perthshire, "was Master of Horses to the Pretender's son at Preston Battle," gone abroad *SHS.8.212*

FORBES, JOHN, younger, in Logierait, cottar, Atholl Brigade, in south and in England *CA.3.303, MR.24*

FORBES, ROBERT, in Moulin, Atholl Brigade, at Culloden (paid listing money) *CA.3.304, MR.24*

FORBES, ROBERT, Captain, of Corse, Duke of Perth's Regiment, taken prisoner Carlisle, acquitted *MR.67*

FORBES, ROBERT, Captain, Duke of Perth's Regiment, son of Newe, deserted, taken prisoner, pardoned *MR.67*

FRASER, HUGH, Captain, son of Fraserdale, Atholl Brigade *CA.3.300, MR.18*

FRASER, HUGH, from Perth, aged 28, blacksmith, Montrose, Ogilvy's Regiment, imprisoned 27.4.1746 Montrose; 13.5.1746 Inverness, June 1746 shipped on *Jane of Leith* to Tilbury Fort, transported 31.3.1747 from London to Jamaica on *St George* or *Carteret* *P.2.212, MR.101, PRO.CO137.28*

GLENY, PETER, weaver, Pittnepy, Coupar Angus, Perthshire, carried arms and after his return from inverury skirmish, surrendered them to Mr Alison of Newhall, at home *SHS.8.214*

GOW, JOHN, servant to Aldie, Auchtergaven, Perthshire, carried arms as a volunteer during the whole rebellion, lurking near home *SHS.8.216*

GOWER, GEORGE, workman, Alyth, Perthshire, carried arms in Lord Ogilvie's regiment, taken prisoner at Carlisle, 30.12.1745, transported 1747 *P.2.244, SHS.8.214*

GRAY, WILLIAM, of Ballegerno, Inchture, Perthshire, imprisoned in Dundee, discharged 17.7.1746 "Was with the rebels at Stirling, now a prisoner in Dundee" *P.2.266, SHS.8.216*

GREIG, DAVID, soldier in Roy Stewart's Regiment, captured at the siege of Carlisle 30 Dec 1745, *CA.3.132*

GREEK, DAVID, servant to Stenton, Caputh, Perthshire, joined army after Preston battle, and continued until their retreat from Stirling, lurking near home *SHS.8.216*

GREENHILL, WILLIAM, gardener from Lethendy, Perthshire, Ogilvy's Regiment, imprisoned 1.7.1746 Perth, 8.8.1746 Canongate, Carlisle, transported. He is said to have "joined the rebel army after Preston battle and continued till after their retreat from Stirling". In the Carlisle return it is stated that he was not brought to trial in Sept 1746 as he was "in hopes of being discharged for want of evidence." He was very ill. His name, however, was shown in Feb 1747 on the transportation lists. No further reference to him *P.2.268, SHS.8.216*

GOW, CHARLES, Croft, Crombie, Glentilt, 2nd Battalion, Atholl Brigade *MR.24*

GOW, DONALD, in Middle Dalguise, Atholl Brigade, in south and in England *CA.3.305, MR.24*

GOW, JOHN, servant to Aldie, Auchtergavin, Atholl Brigade *MR.24*

GOW, PATRICK, in Easter Dalguise (paid listing money), Atholl Brigade, in south and in England *CA.3.305, MR.24*

GOW, THOMAS, Dunkeld, shoemaker *CA.3.307*

GOWER, GEORGE, workman from Alyth, Perthshire, Ogilvy's Regiment, was taken prisoner at the surrender of Carlisle, imprisoned 30.12.1745 Carlisle, transported 1747 *P.2.244*

GRAEME, (or GARVOCK) ROBERT, Lieutenant, of Garvock, Perthshire Horse, "Perthshire Squadron", Viscount, son of William Graham and Christian Graham, imprisoned Perth Tolbooth 1753, released 1754. Escaped after Culloden to Sweden but was arrested on his return to Scotland in 1753. Apparently released in 1754 *P.2.246, MR.53, GS114*

GRAHAM, PETER, Gorthie, Fowls, went along as Commissary, whereabouts not known *SHS.8.44*

GRAHAM, ROBERT, of Garrack, Forteviot, levied the Excise at Duns for the rebels and went along with them, whereabouts not known *SHS.8.44*

GRAHAM, WILLIAM, Perthshire, Kilmarnock's Horse Regiment, *MR.44*

GRANT, DONALD, Whitefield's, Atholl Brigade *MR.24*

GRAY, WILLIAM, surgeon apprentice, Perth, went as volunteer, prisoner in Edinburgh *SHS.8.44*

GREEK, DAVID, serant to Stenton, Caputh, Atholl Brigade *MR.24*

GREENHILL, WILLIAM, gardener in Lethendy, transported 1747 *P.2.268, MR.102*

HADDIN (or HALDANE), JOHN, Major, Perthshire Horse, of Lendrick (or Lanerick), parish of Kilmadock, Perthshire, carried arms in Life Guards, whereabouts not known *SHS.8.56, MR.53*

HAGGART, DAVID, of Cairnmuir, Kirkhill, Caputh, Perthshire, "in a public company wished confusion to His Majesty's Army and success to the rebels," at home. *SHS.8.218*

HALDANE, JOHN, Mr, ?Life Guards, of Lendrick, Kilmadock, Perthshire, imprisoned after Culloden in Cromarty Town House, died of wounds 30.5.1746. "A young gentleman .....died of wounds." *P.2.272*

HALL, WILLIAM, coachbuilder from Perth, imprisoned 7.2.1746 Perth and 1.4.1746 Edinburgh Jail, Carlisle and York Castle, transported. Suspicion of treasonable practices. "Several witnesses saw him making carriages for the rebel's cannon; others state that he attended the Non-Jurant Episcopal Meeting House" *P.2.272*

HAMILTON, ROBERT, Duke of Perth's Regiment, gardener from Gorthie, Perth, imprisoned in Chester Castle, "taken near Leek", presumably on the march into England, transported 5 May 1747 from Liverpool to Virginia in *Johnson*, arrived Port Oxford, Maryland 5 Aug 1747 *P.2.274, MR.72, PRO.T1.328*

HARRELL, WILLIAM, Strothell Miln, Muthill, carried arms as a volunteer, whereabouts not known *SHS.8.46*

HENDERSON, DUNCAN, Lieutenant, merchant in Perth, Atholl Brigade, now lurking *CA.3.300, SHS.8.46, MR.19*

HENDERSON, WILLIAM, Lieutenant, baker, Perth, now lurking *SHS.8.46, MR.53*

HENDERSON, WILLIAM, chapman from Meigle, Ogilvy's Regiment, imprisoned 13.5.1746 Glamis, 24.5.1746 Montrose, Dundee 13.8.1746, released under General Pardon, 1747 *P.2.284*

HILL, THOMAS, brewer, Dunkeld, dead *CA.3.306, SHS.8.46*

HOME, DAVID, labouring man from Bandean, Inchture, Perthshire, carried arms and went to England, prisoner at Carlisle *SHS.8.216*

HUME, JOHN, from Bandean, Inchture, Perthshire, Ogilvy's Regiment, imprisoned 30.12.1745 after siege of Carlisle, and York Castle. No further reference to him *P.2.292, SHS.8.216*

ILLAH, WILLIAM, soldier in Roy Stewart's Regiment, captured at the siege of Carlisle 30 Dec 1745, *CA.3.132*

IRVINE, ALEXANDER, servant to Blair'nrash, Atholl Brigade, killed at Culloden (paid listing money) *CA.3.304, MR.24*

JACK, DAVID, wright, Dunkeld, volunteer, whereabouts not known *CA.3.306, SHS.8.46*

JACK, DAVID, wright from Stratherrol, imprisoned 6.7.1746 Stratherrol, 6.7.1746 Dundee, discharged 16.3.1747 *P.2.298*

JAMIESON, ROBERT, Piper, Annandale, taken prisoner at Carlisle, died? *MR.69*

JOHNSTONE, JAMES, Vintner, Dunkeld, not out; taken prisoner, Feb 1746 *CA.3.300*

KEARNS, JOHN, Captain, aged 42 from Perthshire, imprisoned in Inverness June 1746, shipped on *Jane of Leith* to Tilbury. "Clerk of the rebel's stores". There is no further reference to him *P.2.308*

KEIR, ALEXANDER, Faskally's, 3rd Battalion, Atholl Brigade, deserted Nov 1745 *MR.24*

KEIR, JOHN, in Rotwell, servant (paid listing money), Atholl Brigade, wounded at Culloden *CA.3.303, MR.24*

KENNEDY, ALEXANDER, Craggan, (Lude's), Atholl Brigade, deserted before Preston *MR.24*

KENNEDY, DONALD, Balnacree (Lude's), Atholl Brigade, deserted before Preston *MR.24*

KENNEDY, JOHN, age 32, born 1715, labourer, Rannoch, Perthshire, Keppoch's Regiment, 5'9" tall, black hair, well made. Taken south in May 1746 on board the transport *Jane of Leith,* transported 5 May 1747 from Liverpool to Leeward Islands on *Veteran,* liberated by a French Privateer and landed on Martinique Jun 1747, *P.2.314, PRO.SP36.102,ff.120r-121v, CA.3.316*

KENNEDY, JOHN, age 54, from Perthshire, Keppoch's Regiment, imprisoned Inverness June 1746, shipped on *Jane of Leith* to Tilbury, transported 31 Mar 1747 from London to Jamaica in *St George* or *Carteret,* arrived Jamaica 1747 *P.2.316, MR.163, PRO.CO137.58*

KENNEDY, NEIL, Crofter, Ewen, (Lude's), Atholl Brigade, deserted before Preston, taken prisoner, turned King's Evidence, discharged *MR.24*

KING (or MACREE), ?. 2nd Battalion, Atholl Brigade, taken prisoner, 19.7.46 pardoned *MR.22*

KINLOCH, ALEXANDER, Captain, 2nd Bn Ogilvy's Regiment, aged 28 from Meigle, Perthshire, brother to Sir James Kinloch. Imprisoned 29.4.1746 Bendochy, 1.5.1746 Perth, Inverness June 1746, shipped on *Dolphin* to Winchelsea, London, Newgate, House of Carrington, messenger, liberated on condition of going abroad and never returning 14.8.1748. He was a merchant. He joined the Prince at Perth and received a Captain's commission, and was active in raising the 2nd Battalion of Ogilvy's regiment. He was captured along with his brother at the house of James Rattray of Rannagulzion, and taken by ship to London. He was brought up for trial 28 October and pleaded that under the Act of Union an English court had no jurisdiction over him. This plea was seriously considered, but, on 15 December, it was rejected, and he was sentenced to death. He was reprieved through the exertions of Sir Joseph Yorke, but was kept in custody until 14 August 1748, when he was liberated on condition of "departing this Realm and never more to return." *P.2.322, SHS.8.220*

KINLOCH, CHARLES, Captain, Atholl Brigade (?Ogilvy's), aged 21, from Meigle, Perthshire, imprisoned 29.4.1746 Bendoch, 1.5.1746 Perth, June 1746 shipped on *Dolphin* to Southwark, London, House of Carrington, messenger, reprieved and banished on condition of never returning, 1748. Book-keeper to an Aberdeen merchant. Brother of Sir James Kinloch of Kinloch. Was captured with him and conveyed to Perth, and sent to England. He appears to have taken an active part in raising money and to have pressed men. A petition in his favour was signed by John Chalmers, Principal of King's College, Aberdeen, and the heritors of several neighbouring parishes. He was convicted and sentenced to death, but was reprieved and sent to a messenger's house, where he still was in June 1748. He was then banished on 21 July 1748 *P.2.322, SHS.8.220*

KINLOCH, JAMES, Sir, Bart, of Kinloch, Meigle, Colonel, 2nd Ogilvy's Regiment, imprisoned 29.4.1746 Bendochy, 1.5.1746 Perth,

Inverness, shipped on *Winchelsea* to Southwark (London), House of Carrington, messenger, released conditionally 14.8.1748. On 2 September 1745 the Prince wrote to him from Blair and asked him to join. He raised a second battalion of the Ogilvy Regiment. After his capture he was sent to London, and on 15 November 1746 was attainted and sentenced to death. He refused to give any information about himself when Mr Sharpe, the solicitor to the Treasury, came to question him in prison. He was reprieved through the interest of his brother-in-law, Lord Braco (afterwards Earl of Fife), but remained in custody until 14.8.1748, when he was released on condition that he lived in England. He died there on 5 February 1776 *P.2.324*

KINLOCH, JANET, Lady, of Kinloch, Meigle, Perthshire, imprisoned April 1749, Inverness, London, released. Janet Duff, sister of Lord Braco, afterwards Earl of Fife, was wife of Sir James Kinloch, Bt, who commanded the 2nd Battalion of the Ogilvy Regiment, and was taken prisoner on 29.4.1746. She was herself taken prisoner in April 1746, but discharged. At her husband's request she went to London. It is said that when his life was spared she expressed her gratitude to Sir Joseph Yorke, brother of Lord Hardwicke, for his help. He asked her to name her next child after him; and in due course she called her son Joseph Yorke Kinloch *P.2.324*

LAIRD, DAVID, Lieutenant, Atholl Brigade, *CA.3.300, MR.19*

LAIRD, DAVID, from Perthshire, imprisoned 12.5.1746 in Perth, 10.8.1746 Canongate, Carlisle. "On rebel service." Was tried at Carlisle 19 Sep 1746 and acquitted *P.2.330*

LAIRD, JAMES, born 1721, servant to Murrie, Murrie, Errol, Perthshire, carried arms and was at the battle of Culloden and there taken prisoner, shipped to Tilbury Fort, and transported 31 March 1747 from London to Barbados in *Frere, P.2.330, MR.104, SHS.8.222*

LAIRD, PATRICK, Lieutenant, Vintner, Meigle, Perthshire, Lord Ogilvie's 2nd Battalion, carried arms in England and at the battles of Falkirk and Culloden, now about Glenshoe *SHS.8.222*

LASKEY, JAMES, from Perth, Duke of Perth's Regiment, imprisoned 30.12.1745 after siege of Carlisle. No further reference to him, he may have died *P.2.332, MR.72*

LAWSON, DAVID, servant, Alyth, Perthshire, carried arms in Ogilvie's 1st Battalion and was at the battle of Falkirk, come home *SHS.8.222*

LAWSON, THOMAS, Chapman from Alyth, Perthshire, Ogilvy's Regiment, imprisoned 30.12.1745 Carlisle, Liverpool, pardoned 27.2.1749. He was tried at Carlisle in September 1746, convicted, and sentenced to death. This sentence was ultimately modified to transportation. He tried to escape out of prison. He was sent to Liverpool, where he fell ill and could not be shipped. On 7 January 1749 it was reported he was still ill in prison suffering from stone, and on 27 February 1749 he received a pardon and was released *P.2.334, SHS.8.222*

LAWSON, WILLIAM, Perthshire, Strathallan's Regiment, imprisoned 1.2.1746 Stirling, 7.2.1746 Stirling Castle, 13.2.1746 Leith, discharged. "With the Master of Strathallan," "Tenant of Stralachlan (?Strathallan)" *P.2.336*

LINDSAY, JAMES, shoemaker, Perth, volunteer, prisoner at Inverness *SHS.8.46*

LINDSAY, JAMES, shoemaker apprentice, Perth, seen with the rebels in arms, but said to be forced out, now lurking *SHS.8.46*

LINDSAY, JAMES, shoemaker aged 30 from Perth, Ensign, Strathallan's Regiment, imprisoned 16.4.1746 Culloden, Inverness, shipped June 1746 on *Margaret and Mary* to London (Southwark), pardoned unconditionally. He was second son of David Lindsay of Dowhill. When tried in London on 28 October 1746 he was convicted and sentenced to death, but was reprieved on the way to the scaffold and pardoned on condition that he went abroad "to one of His Majesty's colonies during the term of his natural life." This condition appears to have been withdrawn, as he settled in London as a shoemaker. When he was taken prisoner he is said to have been robbed of his clothing and to have made himself a covering entirely of straw *P.2.342, MR.53, SHS.8.371, SRO.GD.254.1176*

LINDSAY, MARTIN, Writer in Edinburgh, from Perth, acted as Secretary to Lord Strathallan and Oliphant of Gask, imprisoned 16.5.1746 Edinburgh, 17.5.1746 Edinburgh Tolbooth, 8.8.1746 Carlisle, York. He is said to have swallowed down the bitter pill of abjuration" for his religion and "to have escaped being

executed." He was tried at Carlisle (or York), acquitted and
released 26.9.1746 *SHS.8.46, P.2.342, SHS.8.371,
SRO.GD.254.708*

LINDSAY, WILLIAM, wright from Perth, imprisoned 7.2.1746 Perth,
1.4.1746 Edinburgh Jail, discharged. Suspicion of treasonable
practices. "Witnesses state that they saw him viewing the rebel
tranches at Perth with the Governor and others. John Gardiner and
James Campbell say they were employed by the prisoner to cut
down some of the Town of Perth's Fir planting to make pallisades
for the rebels. Other witnesses say he always attended the Non-
Jurant Episcopal Meeting House." *P.2.344*

LIVINGSTON, DONALD, labourer from Perthshire, imprisoned
10.7.1746 Musselburgh, discharged *P.2.346*

LOCKHART, JAMES, wright, Crieff, volunteer in some superior station,
now lurking *SHS.8.46*

LOW, JOHN, Ensign, tenant, Balanluig, killed at Culloden *CA.3.298,
CA.3.300, CA.3.303*

LOW, JOHN, farmer, Ballinluig, Logierait, Ensign, Atholl Brigade, acted
in the character of an officer, now lurking (or killed Culloden)
SHS.8.46, MR.21

LOW, JOHN, New Mill, Strathord, smith *CA.3.307*

LOW, WILLIAM, in Haugh of Killmorich, cottar, (paid listing money),
Atholl Brigade, at Culloden *CA.3.303, MR.24*

LOW, WILLIAM, Sergeant, Chapman, Ballbowna, Forgan, carried arms
in Lord Ogilvie's 2nd Battalion, come home *SHS.8.222*

LYON, ROBERT, Mr, Minister, aged 35, Perth, went along as Army
Chaplain, Ogilvy's Regiment, imprisoned 13.5.1746 Invercarty
Montrose, 15.5.1746 Montrose, 13.8.1746 Canongate, 8.8.1746
Carlisle, executed Penrith, 28.10.1746. Incumbent of the
Episcopal Church in Perth. He joined the Prince when he marched
through to Edinburgh, especially as many of his congregation had
also done so. He was appointed to Lord Ogilvy's regiment, and
served with it throughout the campaign at his own expense.
Although he never bore arms he was found guilty of high treason

and levying war. In his last speech he referred to the denunciation of him by the notorious George Miller, town clerk of Perth, who as responsible for many deaths of Jacobites *SHS.8.46, P.2.354* Was tried at York, found guilty, and executed in November 1746. He is said to have read at the place of execution a lengthy paper, declaring his unswerving attachment to the Jacobite cause. *SHS.8.371*

McALPIN, DONALD, aged 50 from Perth, Duke of Perth's Regiment, imprisoned Inverness, June 1746 shipped on *Wallsgrave* to Tilbury Fort. "Carrier in Sir Robert Clifton's work." No reference to his disposal; probably died *P.3.18*

McARA, ROBERT, in Sock, cottar, Atholl Brigade, in south and in England *CA.3.303, MR.24*

McARTHUR, JOHN, Lieutenant, of Callendar, Duke of Perth's Regiment, imprisoned Callendar 4.5.1746, Stirling Castle, discharged 29.4.1746 *P.3.18, MR.68*

McBAIN, JOHN, aged 18 from Perthshire, McIntosh's Regiment, imprisoned in Inverness June 1746, shipped on *Wallsgrave* to Tilbury, transported 20.3.1747 *P.3.20*

McBAIN, JOHN, aged 49 from Perth, McIntosh's Regiment, imprisoned in Inverness, shipped to Tilbury Fort, transported. Servant to David Michie near Dunkeld *P.3.20*

McBEATH, ARCHIBALD, Clachghlas *CA.3.307*

McBEATH, DONALD, Clachghlas *CA.3.307*

McCARTER, JOHN, soldier in Roy Stewart's Regiment, captured at the siege of Carlisle 30 Dec 1745, *CA.3.132*

McCOLLIE, JAMES, soldier in Roy Stewart's Regiment, captured at the siege of Carlisle 30 Dec 1745, *CA.3.132*

McCOMB (or McCHOMBICH), GILBERT, from Perth, Duke of Perth's Regiment, imprisoned 30.12.1745 after capture at the siege of Carlisle, transported 1747 *P.3.26, MR.73*

McCULLOCH, JAMES, from Perth, soldier in Roy Stewart's (Edinburgh) Regiment, captured at the siege of Carlisle 30 Dec 1745. No further reference to him *CA.3.132, P.3.20, MR.207*

McDANIEL, DANIEL, from Perthshire, Lord George Murray's Regiment, Atholl Brigade, imprisoned 30.12.1745 Carlisle and Liverpool, transported, taken at capture of Carlisle *P.3.32, MR.24*

McDONALD, ALEXANDER, Drumchastle, tenant? (rank unknown), killed, at Culloden (auth. Garth's list) *CA.3.298, CA.3.300*

McDONALD, ALEXANDER, of Dalchosnie, Officer, Atholl Brigade, killed Culloden, *CA.3.298, CA.3.300, CA.3.308, MR.20*

McDONALD, ALEXANDER, servant to Young, Trinafour, Atholl Brigade *MR.24*

McDONALD, ALLAN, brewer, Crieff, volunteer, whereabouts not known *SHS.8.46*

McDONALD, ANGUS, younger of Ceann a Cnoc, Officer, Atholl Brigade, *CA.3.300, MR.20*

McDONALD, ANGUS, in Tullimet, cottar, Atholl Brigade, (paid listing money), killed, at Culloden *CA.3.303, MR.24*

McDONALD, ANGUS, Balnauran *CA.3.306*

McDONALD, ANGUS, of Kennochknock *CA.3.308*

McDONALD, DANIEL, Lettoch Beag, labourer, Lord George Murray's Regiment, captured at the siege of Carlisle, 30 Dec 1745, imprisoned in Chester Castle, Feb 1746.*CA.3.221*

McDONALD, DONALD, in Ballnakeily's ground, (paid listing money), Atholl Brigade, in south and in England, killed *CA.3.305, MR.24*

McDONALD, DONALD, labourer, Lochbeg, Perthshire, 3rd Battalion, Atholl Brigade, taken at Carlisle 30.12.1745, transported 24 Feb 1747 from Liverpool to Virginia in *Gildart*, arriving North Potomac, Maryland 5 Aug 1747 *P.3.56, MR.156, PRO.T1.328, MR.24*

McDONALD, HUGH, aged 30 from Perth, Duke of Perth's Regiment, imprisoned at Inverness June 1746 shipped on *Wallsgrave* to Tilbury. No further reference to him, probably died *P.3.62, MR.73*

McDONALD, JOHN, brother of Alexander McDonald of Dalchosnie, Officer, Atholl Brigade, killed, Culloden *CA.3.300, MR.20*

McDONALD, JOHN, younger, son of Alexander McDonald of Dalchosnie, Officer, soldier in Keppoch's regiment *CA.3.300, CA.3.308*

McDONALD, JOHN, brother of Alexander (rank unknown), killed *CA.3.298*

McDONALD, JOHN, in Dysart (paid listing money), Atholl Brigade, in south and in England, killed *CA.3.305, MR.24*

McDONALD, JOHN, aged 40, from Perthshire, soldier of Lord George Murray's Regiment, 2nd Battalion, Atholl Brigade, captured at siege of Carlisle, 30 Dec 1745, imprisoned in Carlisle and York Castle, transported *CA.3.132, P.3.66, MR.24*

McDONALD, MARGARET, aged 23, born 1724, spinner and knitter, Perthshire, black hair, imprisoned in Lancaster Castle. Variously "discharged" or "transported 5 May 1747 from Liverpool to the Leeward Islands on *Veteran*," which was liberated by a French Privateer and landed on Martinique in Jun 1747 *PRO.SP36.102,ff.120r-121v, P.3.74*

McDONELL, ANGUS, Major, brother of Donald McDonell of Lochgarry, Glengarry's Regiment, wounded, Culloden *CA.3.300*

McDONELL, DONALD, Lieutentant Colonel, of Lochgarry, Glengarry's Regiment, wounded, Clifton *CA.3.300, CA.3.308*

McDOUGALL, ALEXANDER, tenant to Struan, Atholl Brigade, taken prisoner 1745, pardoned *MR.25*

McDOUGALL, ALLAN, (blind), 1st Battalion, Atholl Brigade, taken prisoner 17.1.1746 pardoned *MR.22*

McDOUGALL, DONALD, tenant to Struan, Atholl Brigade, taken prisoner November 1745, discharged *MR.25*

McDOUGALL, JOHN, in Badvo, killed at Culloden (paid listing money), Atholl Brigade *CA.3.304, MR.25*

McDOUGALL, PATRICK, in Ballinluig, killed at Culloden, (paid listing money), Atholl Brigade *CA.3.304, MR.25*

McDUFF, ALEXANDER, brother to Balanloan, Officer, Atholl Brigade *CA.3.300, MR.20*

McDUFF, JAMES, labourer in Ballincreughan, taken prisoner in Carlisle, transported 22 Apr 1747 from Liverpool to Virginia on *Johnson*, landed at Port Oxford, Maryland 5 Aug 1747 *P.3.84, PRO.T1.328, MR.207*

McEWEN, DONALD, mason, Dunkeld, volunteer, now at home *CA.3.306, SHS.8.48*

McEWEN, JOHN, younger of Mucklie, Captain, Grandtully's Regiment, killed Culloden *CA.3.300*

McEWEN, JOHN (1715), Dunkeld, Officer, Atholl Brigade, now lurking *CA.3.300, SHS.8.48, MR.20*

McEWEN, JOHN, Lieutenant, son of the Laird of Dungarthle, Dungarthle, Caputh, Perthshire, joined army before Falkirk battle, whereabouts not known *SHS.8.226*

McEWEN, JOHN, Captain, son of Mucklie, commanding Grandtully's men in Roy Stewart's Regiment, killed *CA.3.298*

McFARLANE, DAVID (or DANIEL), from Perth, Duke of Perth's Regiment, imprisoned 30.12.1745 Carlisle and London, released. Baggage driver. Was forced to enlist. Taken at capture of Carlisle. He turned King's Evidence against other prisoners *P.3.88*

McFARLANE, DONALD, in Cammoch, Atholl Brigade, in south and in England *CA.3.304, MR.25*

McFARLANE, DUNCAN (or DONALD), Baggage Driver, Perth, Duke of Perth's Regiment, taken Carlisle, turned King's Evidence, discharged *MR.73*

McFARLANE, ELIZABETH, aged 30, born 1717, seamstress, Perthshire, 5'8" tall, black hair, lusty, ruddy. Taken at capture of Carlisle, imprisoned 30.12.1745 Carlisle and York Castle, transported 8 May 1747 from Liverpool to Antigua, Leeward Islands on *Veteran*, liberated by a French Privateer, landed Martinique June 1747, *P.3.88, PRO.SP36.102,ff.120r-121v, P.3.88*

McFARLANE, GEORGE, from Menteith, imprisoned in Stirling 2.3.1746, discharged 22.4.1746. Tenant in Callander, on suspicion *P.3.88*

McFARLANE, JAMES from Perth, soldier in Roy Stewart's (Edinburgh) Regiment, captured at the siege of Carlisle 30 Dec 1745, imprisoned in Carlisle and Chester. Nothing more is known of him. He may have died *CA.3.132, P.3.88, MR.207*

McFARLANE, JAMES, from Perthshire, Lord John Drummond's Regiment, imprisoned 21.6.1746 in Perth, discharged on bail 21.7.1746 *P.3.88*

McFARLANE, JAMES, Perthshire, Royal Scots Regiment, taken prisoner, discharged *MR.63*

McFARLANE, JOHN, from Strathbraan or Grandtully, soldier in Roy (Edinburgh) Stewart's Regiment, captured at the siege of Carlisle, 30 Dec 1745, died? *CA.3.132, MR.207*

McFARLANE, JOHN, tailor, Dunkeld, joined army on their retreat northwards, absconding *CA.3.306, SHS.8.48*

McFARLANE, JOHN, parish of Little Dunkeld, Lord John Drummond's French Regiment *CA.3.307*

McFARLANE, JOHN, servant, Glenfinglas parish of Callander, was in England and at the battle of Culloden, now lurking *SHS.8.56*

McFARLANE, JOHN, labourer in Denmore, Perth, Roy Stuart's (Edinburgh) Regiment, imprisoned 30.12.1745 Carlisle, Chester Castle, taken at capture of Carlisle. Drowned at Liverpool when going on board a ship for transportation, March 1747 *P.3.88, MR.207*

McFARLANE, JOHN, Perthshire, Roy Stuart's Regiment, imprisoned 30.12.1746 Carlisle after siege of town. No more is known of him *P.3.88*

McGHIE, ...? of Shirloch, Rannoch, Colonel, Robertson's Regiment, Captain in Atholl Brigade, imprisoned 16.1.1746 Culloden, Inverness. Shown in the list of captured officers as "leader of the Rannachs." Nothing more is known of him. He does not appear to have reached London *P.3.90, MR.18*

McGLASHAN, JOHN, in Drum of Pitlochry, Atholl Brigade, in south and in England (paid listing money) *CA.3.304, MR.25*

McGLASHAN, NEIL, Writer, Lieutenant, Alltclune, Atholl Brigade, *CA.3.300, CA.3.308, MR.19*

McGLASHAN, PATRICK, Lieutenant, of Baluain or Lambtown, Atholl Brigade, nephew of Neil McGlashan *CA.3.300, CA.3.308, MR.20*

McGREGOR, (or MURRAY) DUNCAN, Captain, brother of Robert McGregor of Glencarnock, wounded, Prestonpans *CA.3.300*

McGREGOR, (or MURRAY) DUNCAN, Wester Drumlich, Balquhidder *CA.3.307*

McGREGOR, DUNCAN, of Roro, Officer, Atholl Brigade, *MR.20*

McGREGOR, DUNCAN, transported 22 Apr 1747 from Liverpool to Virginia on *Johnson*, landed Port Oxford, Maryland, 5 Aug 1747 *PRO.T1.328*

McGREGOR, DUNCAN, aged 17, of Breadalbane, Lord John Murray's Regiment, imprisoned 24.6.1746 Perth, 9.8.1746 Carlisle. "Denies being concerned in the rebellion. There is a letter from Sir Patrick Murray, the prisoner's captain, declaring that he was not concerned in the rebellion." Was tried at Carlisle 19 Sept 1746 and acquitted. *P.3.92*

McGREGOR, (or MURRAY) EVAN, Major, brother to Robert McGregor of Glencarnock, ADC to Prince *CA.3.300*

McGREGOR, (or MURRAY) GREGOR, Captain, Atholl Brigade, Coinneachan, Glenalmond, taken prisoner Feb 1746, *CA.3.300, MR.19*

McGREGOR-MURRAY, GREGOR JOHN, of Glengyle, governor of Doune Castle, taken prisoner 15.4.1746 *MR.167*

McGREGOR, (or CAMPBELL) JAMES, from Crieff, piper in MacGregor's Regiment, taken prisoner at Carlisle, transported 21 Nov 1748, *P.2.94, MR.167*

McGREGOR, JOHN, labourer, Dundurn, Perthshire, Duke of Perth's Regiment, taken after siege of Carlisle 30.12.1745, transported 22 Apr 1747 from Liverpool to Virginia on *Johnson*, landed at Port Oxford, Maryland 5 Aug 1747, *P.3.94, MR.73, PRO.T1.328*

McGREGOR, (or MURRAY) JOHN, Monachyle, Balquhidder, Keppoch's Regiment, *CA.3.307*

McGREGOR, JOHN, labourer, Perthshire, Duke of Perth's Regiment, taken prisoner, executed 8.11.1746 *MR.74*

McGREGOR, JOHN, labourer, Perthshire, Duke of Perth's Regiment, taken prisoner, transported 22 Apr 1747 from Liverpool to Maryland, in *Johnson* arriving Port Oxford, Maryland, 5 Aug 1747 *MR.74, P.3.94, PRO.T.1.328*

McGREGOR, (or DRUMMOND), JOHN, Balnacuik, Balquhidder, nephew to Balhaldie, Commandant at Crieff, taken prisoner, transported 1747 *P.2.164, MR.167*

McGREGOR, JOHN, of Learagan, Officer, Atholl Brigade *MR.20*

McGREGOR, (or MURRAY) MALCOLM, of Craigruie, Balquhidder, Captain Duke of Perth's Regiment, wounded, Prestonpans *CA.3.300*

McGREGOR, JOHN, labourer, Perthshire, imprisoned 13.-.1746 Perth, 9.8.1746 Carlisle, York Castle. Pleaded guilty at his trial at York on 2 Oct 1746 and was sentenced to death, executed 8.11.1746 York *P.3.94*

McGREGOR, MALCOLM, Lieutenant, of Liaran (Shian's), Atholl
Brigade *MR.20*

McGREGOR, MARK, aged 24 (born 1723) from Balnagowan Perth,
cook, Baggot's Hussars Regiment, imprisoned 28.2.1746 Perth,
10.8.1746 Canongate, Carlisle, transported 24 Feb 1747 from
Liverpool to Virginia on *Gildart*, landed Port North Potomac,
Maryland, 5 Aug 1747, *P.3.96, MR.40, PRO.T1.328, P.3.96*

McGREGOR, MARY, Balquhidder, Perthshire, Keppoch's Regiment,
imprisoned in Carlisle and Chester Castle, discharged. Nothing
more is known of her *P.3.96*

McGREGOR (or MURRAY), PATRICK, farmer, Easter Drumlich,
Balquhidder, Keppoch's Regiment, transported 22 Apr 1747 from
Liverpool to Virginia on *Johnson*, landed Port Oxford, Maryland, 5
Aug 1747, *P.3.220, PRO.T1.328, CA.3.307*

McGREGOR (or MURRAY), PATRICK, Perthshire, Glengyle's
Regiment, imprisoned 12.5.1746 Perth, 9.8.1746 Carlisle. Was
tried at Carlisle 19/26 Sept 1746 and acquitted *P.3.96*

McGREGOR (or MURRAY), ROBERT, Lieutenant Colonel, of
Glencarnock, Balquhidder, McGregor's Regiment, *CA.3.300*

McGREGOR (or MURRAY), ROBERT, of Ardlarich, Captain, 1st
Battalion Atholl Brigade *CA.3.330, MR.18*

McGRIGOR, ALEXANDER ROY, labouring man, Callander was at
Culloden battle, said to be forced, now at home *SHS.8.58*

McGRIGOR, ALEXANDER, tradesman, Miltoun parish of Callander,
carried arms in England, said to be forced, returned home *SHS.8.58*

McGRIGOR, DOUGAL, tradesman, Miltoun, parish of Callander, carried
arms in England, said to be forced, returned home *SHS.8.58*

McGRIGOR, JOHN, labourer, Perthshire, Duke of Perth's Regiment,
imprisoned Oct 1745 Bridge of Allan, 31.10.1745 Stirling Castle,
17.3.1746 Edinburgh Castle, 9.8.1746 Carlisle. "On suspicion".
Transported 22 Apr 1747 from Liverpool to Maryland on *Johnson*
arriving Port Oxford, Maryland 5 Aug 1747 *P.3.94, MR74,
PRO.T1.328*

McGRIGOR, PATRICK, tradesman, Miltoun parish of Callander, carried arms into England, said to be forced, returned home *SHS.8.58*

McGROUTHER, ALEXANDER, Lieutenant, aged 30, from Perthshire, Duke of Perth's Regiment, captured at siege of Carlisle, 30 Dec 1745. According to Sir John Stranger's papers, he "died before trial." *CA.3.131, P.3.98, MR.68*

McGROUTHER, ALEXANDER, Lieutenant, aged 76, from Dalchruinn, Duke of Perth's Regiment, taken prisoner 30.12.1745 Carlisle, pardoned *MR.68*

McHUMISH, JOHN, pedlar, Bridge of Turk, parish of Callander, was at Falkirk and Culloden battles, now lurking *SHS.8.58*

McINHONNEL, JOHN, Sergeant, brewer, Bridge of Kelty, parish of Callander, returned home *SHS.8.58*

McINROY, JAMES, in Easter Cluny, Atholl Brigade, in south and in England *CA.3.304, MR.25*

MacINTYOUNGERE, ANGUS, Perthshire, baggageman, deserted, taken prisoner November 1745, pardoned *MR.165*

McKENZIE, DANIEL, Perth, Duke of Perth's Regiment, taken prisoner with his wife (Ann McKenzie, aged 60? *P.3.114*) 30.12.1745 after siege of Carlisle, also imprisoned in Lancaster Castle, transported 1747 *P.3.116, MR.74*

Mackintosh, JAMES, in Craig'nuisk, in south and in England *CA.3.303*

McINTOSH, ALEXANDER, born 1678, labourer from Balnabroich, Strathardle, transported 24 Feb 1747 from Liverpool to Virginia on *Gildart*, landed at Port North Potomac, Maryland, 5 Aug 1747, *P.3.100, PRO.T1.328, MR.74, CA.3.307*

McINTOSH, JAMES, Craig n'nish, Atholl Brigade *MR.25*

McINTOSH, ROBERT, in Glenalbert, Atholl Brigade, in south and in England, (paid listing money) *CA.3.304, MR.25*

McINTYOUNGERE, ALEXANDER, merchant, Keltney Burn,
Fortingall or Dull, Atholl Standard-bearer, whereabouts not known
CA.3.300, SHS.8.46, MR.22

McINTYOUNGERE, ANGUS, labourer from Perthshire, Keppoch's
Regiment, imprisoned 1.2.1746 Stirling, 17.3.1746 Edinburgh
Castle, 13.12.1746 Edinburgh Jail from Castle, released under
General Pardon, 1747. "Says that the rebels forced him to go with
them to Carlisle as a baggage man, and that he left them there."
This statement does not tally with the fact that he was captured at
Stirling during the operations *P.3.104*

McKENZIE, DANIEL, from Perth, Duke of Perth's Regiment, taken at
capture of Carlisle, with his wife, imprisoned 30.12.1745 Carlisle,
Lancaster Castle, transported from Liverpool on *Elizabeth*, Captain
Daniel Cole, 6.2.1748 to Jamaica, but landed on Antigua
21.3.1748. *P.3.116, PRO.T53.44*

McKENZIE, DUNCAN, brother of John McKenzie of Buidh nan Culloch
CA.3.300

McKENZIE, JAMES, Kincraigie *CA.3.307*

McKENZIE, JOHN, of Ruidh nan Culloch (Rinakylach) *CA.3.300,
CA.3.308*

McKENZIE, THOMAS, of Rinakylach *CA.3.308*

McKENZIE, WILLIAM, Perth's Regiment, shipped on *Jane of Leith*,
and died on the ship 3.6.1746 *P.1.188*

McKINLAY, DONALD, Horse Hirer from Perth, imprisoned 17.2.1746
Perth, 1.4.1746 Edinburgh, 8.8.1746 Carlisle. "There is proof that
(along with five sheriff officers of Perth) he ran errands for the
rebels, and went at their desire to warn in carts and horses from the
country to carry their baggage." There is no further reference to
him, and he may have died in prison *P.3.136*

McKINNON, (or McARRON or McKERROW) JANET, spinner from
Perth aged 16, imprisoned 30.12.1745 in Carlisle and Lancaster,
transported 1747. Taken at capture of Carlisle *P.3.18*

McLACHLAN, DONALD, Kincraigie *CA.3.307*

McLACHLAN, JOHN, West Monzie *CA.3.307*

McLACHLAN, JOHN ROY, brewer, Callander, went to Edinburgh, took the benefit of the Indemnity in November 1746, now at home *SHS.8.58*

McLAREN, ALEXANDER, Lieutenant, younger of Easthaugh, Atholl Brigade, *CA.3.300, MR.20*

McLAREN, ARCHIBALD, farmer, Curnoch, assisted with money being forced thereto, or to send a man, now at home *SHS.8.58*

McLAREN, ARRATT, Lieutenant, Uncle to McLaren younger of Esthaugh, Atholl Brigade *MR.20*

McLAREN, DONALD, Captain, drover of Invernentie, Balquhidder, in Appin Stewart's Regiment, imprisoned 19.7.1746 Braes of Leny, Stirling, Edinburgh, Canongate, escaped Aug 1746. He was captured, with some others, while living in a hut in the Braes of Leny. Defending himself he was wounded in the thigh. "When on his way to Carlisle strapped to a dragoon, he cut the strap, threw himself over a cliff and escaped. This incident occurred on Erickstane Brae at the hollow formerly called Annandale's Beefstand but now McLaren's Leap." After his escape he went back to his own country and remained in disguise until the Act of Indemnity *P.3.142*

McLAREN, DONALD, in Dowally, tenant, Atholl Brigade, wounded at Culloden *CA.3.303, MR.25*

McLAREN, DONALD, East Kinnaird *CA.3.307*

McLAREN, DUNCAN, Lieutenant, aged 40, brewer from Wester Innernenty, Balquhidder, Tullibardine's Regiment (Duke of Atholl's), imprisoned 10.8.1746 Canongate, released under General Pardon, 1747 *CA.3.300, P.3.166, MR.20*

McLAREN, DUNCAN, Blair Atholl *CA.3.306*

McLAREN, DUNCAN, Perthshire, Duke of Atholl's Regiment, 3rd Battalion, imprisoned 13.6.1746 Perth, 9.8.1746 Carlisle, transported 1747 *P.3.142, MR.25*

McLAREN, JAMES, in Haugh of Killmorich, servant, Atholl Brigade, (paid listing money), at Culloden *CA.3.303, MR.25*

McLAREN, JOHN, in Rotwell, cottar, Atholl Brigade, (paid listing money) wounded at Culloden *CA.3.303, MR.25*

McLAREN, LAWRENCE, servant to "Old Gask", Perthshire Horse, (Strathallan's Regiment), imprisoned 7.5.1746 Perth, discharged on bail July 1746. "On suspicion" *P.3.142, MR.54*

McLAUCHLAN, ALEXANDER, Major, in Ladhill, Atholl Brigade, taken prisoner at Culloden, escaped *MR.18*

McLAUGHLANE, WILLIAM in Logierait, cottar, Atholl Brigade, in south and in England *CA.3.303, MR.25*

McLEAN, ALEXANDER, shoemaker apprentice, Perth, seen in arms but said to be pressed, now lurking *SHS.8.46*

McLEAN, ALEXANDER, Sergeant, brewer, Long Loggie, Meigle, Perthshire, at the battles of Falkirk and Culloden, whereabouts not known *SHS.8.226*

McLEAN, ANTHONY, East Downie, Strathardle *CA.3.307*

McLEAN, OWEN (?EWEN), weaver of Tullohghallan, Strathearn, Perthshire, Glenbucket' Regiment, imprisoned 30.12.1745 Carlisle, Chester Castle. Taken at capture of Carlisle, transported 1747 *P.3.150*

McLEISH, ARCHIBALD, labourer from Breadalbane, imprisoned June 1746 Leith; 25.6.1746 Canongate, discharged 16.3.1747. "In the rebellion." "Says the rebels forced him to drive their baggage." *P.3.152.*

McLEISH, DONALD, servant in Ballnamuir, Atholl Brigade, in south and in England *CA.3.303, MR.25*

McLEISH, DUNCAN, aged 18, born 1729, pedlar, Perthshire, 5" tall, pale complexion, slender, Duke of Perth's Regiment, Struan's Company, imprisoned 5.11.1745 Edinburgh Castle, 15.1.1746 Edinburgh Jail, Carlisle, Lincoln Castle. Ill in hospital, fever and rheumatism. Transported 8 May 1747 from Liverpool to Antigua, Leeward Islands on *Veteran*, liberated by a French Privateer and landed on Martinique Jun 1747, *P.3.152, MR.74, PRO.SP36.102,ff.120r-121v*

McLEISH, JOHN, weaver in Port, cottar, Atholl Brigade, in south and in England *CA.3.303, MR.25*

McLEISH, JOHN, Muthill, carried arms, pressed out and returned home *SHS.8.48*

McLENNAN, HECTOR, aged 40, from Perth, Duke of Perth's Regiment, imprisoned Inverness June 1746, shipped on *Margaret and Mary* to Tilbury. Not transported, may have died at Tilbury *P.3.154*

McLEOD, KENNETH, Perth's Regiment, shipped on *Alexander & James* and died on ship 17.5.1746 *P.1.188*

McNAB, DONALD, farmer, Brae Leing, parish of Callander, first went south and thereafter north, whereabouts not known *SHS.8.58*

McNAB, JOHN, aged 67, labourer from Perth, 3rd Battalion, Atholl's Regiment, imprisoned 7.2.1746 Stirling Castle, 17.3.1746 Edinburgh Castle, 8.8.1746 Carlisle, transported from Liverpool to Virginia in *Johnson*, arrived Port Oxford, Maryland 5 Aug 1747 *P.3.170, MR.25, PRO.T1.328*

McNAB, LEONARD, from Perthshire, 3rd Battalion, Atholl's Regiment, servant to Charles Spalding of Whitefield, imprisoned 3.6.1746 Perth, 10.8.1746 Canongate, 9.8.1746 Carlisle. Fate unknown, was not transported, and probably died *P.3.170, MR.25*

McNAB, THOMAS, in Logierait, cottar, Atholl Brigade, in south and in England *CA.3.303, MR.25*

McNAUGHTON, JOHN, Quartermaster, son of Culdares' Ground Officer, from Glenlyon, Perthshire, in Kilmarnock's Regiment (Perthshire Squadron (Duke of Perth's)), imprisoned 1.7.1746 Perth, 10.8.1746 Canongate, Aug 1746 Carlisle. Servant of Menzies of Culdares. Watchmaker in Edinburgh. "Was at Preston battle and boasted that he had killed Colonel Gardner there." He tried to get Murray of Broughton, who was then in the Tower, to prove that he did not kill Col Gardner. Early in 1745 he was sent by Murray of Broughton to France with the letter from the leaders of the party to the Prince urging him to delay his coming. He returned at the end of May and reported that the Prince would be in South Uist in July. Among other charges brought against him was that he had brought a charger to the Prince. This horse had been sent by James Menzies of Culdares and Meggenie who had been out in the '15. When questioned as to the source of the gift McNaughton absolutely refused to say. Dr Blaikie points out that every effort was made to induce him to give evidence, and on his way to be hanged he was offered his life and a pension if he would do so. He replied that the Government had honoured him in ranking him with gentlemen, and he hoped they would leave him in quiet to suffer as one. He became known as "MacNeachdain an eich a udhir." Executed 18.10.1746 *P.3.172, CA.3.301, MR.54*

McNEIL, PATRICK, from Perthshire, soldier in Roy Stewart's Regiment, captured at the siege of Carlisle 30 Dec 1745 and imprisoned in Carlisle. Nothing more known of him *CA.3.132, P.3.174*

McNEIL, PATRICK, from Perth, in Roy Stuart's (Edinburgh) Regiment, imprisoned 30.12.1745 Carlisle. Taken at capture of Carlisle. Nothing more is know about him *P.3.174, MR.207*

McPHERSON, JAMES, in Kinhaird, Atholl Brigade, (paid listing money), in south and in England *CA.3.304, MR.25*

McQUEEN, ALEXANDER, from Comrie, Perthshire, 3rd Battalion, Duke of Atholl's Regiment, imprisoned 10.6.1746 Perth, discharged on bail 31.7.1746. "On suspicion." *P.3.180, MR.25*

McRAE, DANIEL, Fonnab, Atholl Brigade *MR.25*

McRAE, DAVID, in Fonnab, in south and in England, (paid listing money) *CA.3.305*

McRAW, DONALD, aged 48, from Perth, Lord George Murray's Regiment, 2nd Battalion, Atholl Brigade, imprisoned Inverness June 1746, shipped on *Alexander and James*, transported 1747. This is perhaps the Captain MacRaw, one of the Kintail Macraes, referred to by Dr Blaikie as in Glengarry's Regiment *P.3.182*

McROBBIE, JOHN, younger, of Drummond, Muthill, Perthshire, Duke of Perth's Regiment, went as a volunteer, taken prisoner at Culloden *SHS.8.48, MR.74*

McROBBIE, LEWIS, Drummond *SHS.8.48*

MALCOLM, JAMES, Ground Officer to Perth, 2nd Battalion, Atholl Brigade, taken prisoner, discharged *MR.20*

MALLOCH, JOHN, from Perth, imprisoned 7.4.1747 at Perth, discharged on bail 16.5.1747 "on suspicion" *P.3.6*

MANN, JAMES, born 1727, baker, Dunkeld, Ensign, Roy Stewart's (Edinburgh) Regiment, taken prisoner at Carlisle 30 Dec 1745, also imprisoned in York Castle and Lincoln Castle, pale complexion, well made, transported 8 May 1747 from Liverpool to Antigua, Leeward Islands, on the *Veteran*, liberated by a French Privateer and landed Martinique, June 1747, *P.3.6, MR.205, CA.3.300, CA.3.306, SHS.8.48, PRO.SP36.102,ff.120r-121v*

MANN, JOHN, shoemaker, deserted before Prestonpans, now at home *CA.3.306, SHS.8.48*

MANN, LEONARD, Kincraigie *CA.3.307*

MANN, THOMAS, born 1705, son of James Mann, Writer in Dunkeld, educated at University of St Andrews, minister of Dunkeld 1732-1785, suspended in 1747 as a suspected Jacobite, died 2 Apr 1785 *F.4.155*

MANNOCH, JOHN, in Dunchastle, killed, at Culloden (paid listing money) Atholl Brigade, *CA.3.304, MR.24*

MARR, JAMES, baker from Dunkeld, Glenbucket's Regiment, carried arms. England. Prisoner. No further reference to him in any of the State Papers *P.3.8*

MARSHALL, DONALD, soldier in Roy Stewart's (Edinburgh) Regiment, captured at the siege of Carlisle 30 Dec 1745, also imprisoned in Chester Castle, died in prison *CA.3.132, P.3.8, MR.206*

MARTIN, JOHN, no employment, Perth, volunteer, now lurking
SHS.8.46

MATTHEW (Mathews or Mathy), ANDREW, aged 32, born 1715,
maltster, Perthshire, 5'5" tall, dark complexion, sickly, Duke of
Perth's Regiment, imprisoned in Carlisle, Lincoln and York Castle,
transported 8 May 1747 from Liverpool to the Leeward Islands on
Veteran, liberated by a French Privateer in Martinique Jun 1747,
P.3.12, MR.73, PRO.SP36.102,ff.120r-121v

MENZIES, ...?, of Sheen, acted in the character of an officer,
whereabouts not known *SHS.8.46*

MENZIES, ADAM, from Perthshire, 3rd Battalion, Duke of Atholl's
Regiment, imprisoned 19.3.1746 Stirling, discharged 11.4.1746.
Tenant to Sir Robert Menzies. In the rebellion. *P.3.188, MR.25*

MENZIES, ARCHIBALD, Lieutenant Colonel, of Shian, Colonel, 1st
Battalion, Atholl Brigade, Commanding Weem's men, killed
Culloden *CA.3.298, CA.3.300, MR.18*

MENZIES, JAMES, of Bolfracks, Officer, Atholl Brigade *CA.3.300,
MR.20*

MENZIES, JAMES, of Woodend, Officer, Atholl Brigade *CA.3.300,
MR.20*

MENZIES, JOHN, son of late innkeeper, St Ninian's, Stirling,
Paymaster, Weem's men *CA.3.300, MR.22*

MENZIES, ROBERT, farmer from Callander, Ogilvy's Regiment,
imprisoned 30.3. 1746 Stirling, discharged 29.4.1746. "On
suspicion." *P.3.188*

MENZIES, WALTER, aged 18, born 1729, a flaxdresser from Atholl,
5'3" tall, dark complexion, sickly, soldier of Lord Ogilvie's
Regiment, captured at the siege of Carlisle 30 Dec 1745,
imprisoned in Carlisle and Lincoln Castle, transported 8 May 1747
from Liverpool to Antigua, Leeward Islands on *Veteran*, liberated
by a French Privateer in Martinique Jun 1747, *P.3.188, MR.106,
PRO.SP36.102,ff120r.121v, CA.3.132*

MENZIES, WILLIAM, Lieutenant or Ensign, son of Robert Menzies, Glassie, a surgeon, Atholl Brigade, Weem's men *CA.3.300, MR.20*

MERCER, THOMAS, Lieutenant or Ensign, son (a boy) of Hon Robert Mercer of Aldie, Atholl Brigade, killed Culloden, *CA.3.298, CA.3.299, MR.20*

MERCER, LAURENCE, Mr, of Lethendy, Pendreich, Perthshire Horse, (Strathallan's Regiment), carried arms from a little before Falkirk battle to their dispersing, taken prisoner in Dundee prison, died in prison *MR.54, SHS.8.226*

MERCER, ROBERT, Hon Colonel, of Aldie, brother to Lord Nairne, at first Colonel 3rd Battalion, afterwards a Volunteer, killed, Culloden *CA.3.298, CA.3.299, MR.18*

MERCER, ROBERT, Captain, of Aldie, Meikleour, Caputh, Perthshire, "acted as Captain in the rebel army during the whole rebellion," whereabouts not known *SHS.8.226*

MILLER, ALEXANDER, Benvie, servant to Lord George Murray, 2nd Battalion, Atholl Brigade *CA.3.306, MR.26*

MILLER, JAMES, innkeeper, brewer, Five Mile House, Auchtergaven, Perthshire, imprisoned in Perth, released under General Pardon, 1747. "Was in the mob at Perth on the anniversary of His Majesty's birthday, fired on the townspeople, and active in raising Lord Nairn's tenants into the Rebellion." *CA.3.306, P.3.194, SHS.8.226*

MILLER, JAMES, brewer, Coupar Angus, Perthshire, joined the rebels at Dunkeld on their way south and was very oppressive, now in Glenshoe *SHS.8.224*

MILLER, JOHN, Logiealmond, Duke of Atholl's Regiment, imprisoned 2.7.1746 Perth, discharged 16.3.1747. Gardener at Balmanno. On suspicion. "Confesses that he carried arms on behalf of his brother, who is a tenant to Logiealmond and forced him out. Others saw him in arms with the rebels but say that he soon left them." *P.3.194, MR.25*

MILLER (or MILN), WILLIAM, waggoner from Dunkeld, a boy of 14 years, Duke of Perth's Regiment, Struan's Company, imprisoned

12.5.1746 Perth, discharged on bail 18.3.1747. On suspicion.
"Says that one Gow, a rebel, did partly by force and partly by
flattering carry him north with the rebels. Witnesses declared that
they say him with the rebel army sometimes carrying a knapsack
and other times driving a cart, but never bearing arms." *CA.3.307,
P.3.196, MR.74*

MITCHELL, WALTER, Ensign, Duke of Perth's Regiment, captured at
siege of Carlisle, 30 Dec 1745 *CA.3.131*

MONCRIEFF, THOMAS, late Excise Officer, Perth, Perthshire Horse,
(Strathallan's Regiment), acted as Depute Collector of Excise for
the rebels, probably carried the Squadron's standard at Culloden),
now lurking *SHS.8.46, MR.55*

MONRO, GEORGE, from Perthshire, 3rd Battalion, Duke of Atholl's
Regiment, imprisoned 10.12.1746 Perth, discharged on bail
27.12.1746 *P.3.206, MR.26*

MURDOCH, WILLIAM, Ensign, wool merchant, Callander, thrice
forced out and as often deserted, now at home *SHS.8.58*

MURDOCH, WILLIAM, aged 40, born 1707, wool merchant, Callander,
"Ensign in the Rebel Army," imprisoned Canongate, 8.8.1746
Carlisle. "Acted as ensign in the Rebel Army, was thrice forced
out and as often deserted." Transported 22 Apr 1747 from
Liverpool to Virginia on *Johnson*, landed at Port Oxford,
Maryland, 5 Aug 1747 *P.3.216, PRO.T1.328*

MURRAY – see McGREGOR

MURRAY, ...?, younger of Dollairie, Crieff, volunteer, whereabouts not
known *SHS.8.48*
Mr Murray of Dollary, Sheriff-Depute of Perthshire, is mentioned,
on the occasion of the arrival of the Chevalier at Perth, as having
left that town along with the officers of the revenue. It is
doubtless his son who is named in the List. *SHS.8.372*

MURRAY, ALEXANDER, Captain, of Soilzarie (Dollar), Atholl
Brigade *CA.3.300, MR.19*

MURRAY (or McGREGOR), DUNCAN, from Perthshire, Glengyle's
Regiment, imprisoned 10.8.1746 Canongate, Carlisle, acquitted
26.9.1746 *P.3.216*

MURRAY, GEORGE, Lord (1715, '19) Lieutenant General, 5th son of 1st
Duke, 2nd Battalion Atholl Brigade, escaped abroad *CA.3.299,*
MR.18

MURRAY, GEORGE, Lord, brother to Duke of Atholl, Tullibardine,
Blackford, General *SHS.8.46*
Younger son of John, first Duke of Atholl. He was implicated in
the Spanish enterprise on behalf of the Pretender in 1719, which
ended with the skirmish at Glenshiel in June of that year. He then
escaped abroad, and was some years an officer in the army of the
King of Sardinia; but, having obtained a pardon, he returned, and
was presented to George I. When the standard of rebellion was
again unfurled in 1745, Lord George yielded to the temptation, and
accepted the chief command of the Pretender's forces. In this
position he greatly distinguished himself as a skilful leader and
intrepid soldier. Upon the disastrous conclusion of the campaign
he withdrew to the Continent, and died in Holland in 1760. A
liferent provision which he had out of the estate of Glencarse was
forfeited. His eldest son, John, born in 1729, succeeded as third
Duke of Atholl in 1764. *SHS.8.371*

MURRAY, JOHN, Lord Nairne, Brigadier General, 1st Battalion, Atholl
Brigade, escaped *MR.18*

MURRAY, MUNGO, younger, son of Patrick Murray of Kincairny,
Caputh, Secretary to Duke William, Marquis of Tullibardine,
Atholl Brigade, "joined the rebels a little after their coming to
Dunkeld," escaped to Edinburgh disguised as a woman *CA.3.300,*
MR.22, SHS.8.226

MURRAY, PATRICK, of Kincairny, not out, taken prisoner Feb 1746
CA.3.300

MURRAY, (or McGREGOR) PATRICK (or PETER), farmer, Perthshire,
Glengyle's Regiment, imprisoned Aberdeen, 10.8.1746 Canongate,
Carlisle. Transported 22 Apr 1747 from Liverpool to Virginia on
Johnson, landed at Port Oxford, Maryland 5Aug 1747 *P.3.220,*
PRO.T1.328

MURRAY, ROBERT, alias McGregor, of Glencarnock *CA.3.308*

MURRAY, WILLIAM, Hon, of Taymount, brother to Dunmore, 1st cousin to Duke, volunteer in Army, surrendered, pled guilty, received a pardon *CA.3.299*

MURRAY, WILLIAM, Marquis of Tullibardine (Jacobite Duke of Atholl) Lieutenant General 3rd Battalion, Atholl Brigade, taken and died in Tower of London 9.7.1746 *MR.18*

MURRAY, WILLIAM, Postmaster, Crieff, carried arms in some superior station, whereabouts not known *SHS.8.46*

NAIRN, HENRY, Hon, son of Lord Nairne, Officer, French service, surrendered prisoner after Culloden? *CA.3.299*

NAIRN, JOHN, Lord, (1715), Auchtergaven, Stanley, Perthshire, Colonel, 1st cousin to Duke William, Brigadier General, 1st Battalion, in arms during the whole rebellion, escaped abroad *CA.3.299, SHS.8.226*

NAIRN, THOMAS, Hon, son of Lord Nairne, Officer, French service, taken prisoner at sea, Nov 1745 *CA.3.299*

NAPIER, JOHN, mason, guarded Inver Ferry, now at home *CA.3.306, SHS.8.48*

NEIL, THOMAS, servant to John Stewart of Stenton, Caputh, a volunteer in rebel army. In arms from their coming to Perth to their retreat from Stirling, whereabouts not known *CA.3.306, MR.26, SHS.8.226*

NEISH, JOHN, Perthshire, "In rebel service." Imprisoned 2.5.1746 Perth, discharged on bail March 1747. Servant to Fletcher of Bonshaw. He was one of the Prince's grooms, and appears to have turned King's Evidence against his fellow-prisoners *P.3.224*

NICHOL, THOMAS, workman, Dunkeld, took prisoner excise officer and beat him, absconding *CA.3.306, SHS.8.48*

NICHOLS, ISOBEL, Duke of Perth's Regiment, released 1747, *P.1.217*

NICHOLSON, JAMES, Lieutenant, Duke of Perth's Regiment, captured and executed after siege of Carlisle, 30 Dec 1745 *CA.3.131*

OGILVIE, THOMAS, Captain, of Rienavey or Rilnarey, Atholl Brigade, *CA.3.301, CA.3.308, MR.19*

OLDHAM (OLDHORN), WILLIAM, Perth's Regiment, drowned, Liverpool 2.5.1746 *P.1.188*

OLIPHANT, JAMES, merchant in Perth, imprisoned 7.2.1746 Perth, Edinburgh Castle, 1.4.1746 Edinburgh Jail from Castle, discharged on bail 10.5.1747. On suspicion of treason. "Henry Edwards did see him upon the King's birthday walking through the Rebel guardroom at Perth with a firelock and bayonet and heard some of the rebels call him Captain. Others say they saw him with the rebels under command of Oliphant of Gask disperse the loyal inhabitants of Perth who were solemnising His Majesty's birthday. Others say they frequently saw him walking with the Pretender's son and John McColly says he came to his house with armed highlanders and forced from him one of his horses for the Rebels use." *P.3.242*

OLIPHANT, LAURANCE, Captain, younger of Gask, volunteer, Perthshire Horse, whereabouts not known *SHS.8.48, MR.53*

OLIPHANT, LAURANCE, elder of Gask. The estates of the elder and younger were confiscated; but, in 1753, Mrs Amelia Nairne, spouse to Lawrence Oliphant, lat of Gask, was found entitled to her liferent of portions of the estate, in terms of her marriage contract, in the event of her surviving her husband. On 24 February 1754 he is mentioned as deceased. The daughter of the younger Lawrence, named Carolina, was married to Lord Nairne, and is celebrated as the writer of "The Laird of Cockpen" and other favourite songs *SHS.8.372*

ORR, DUNCAN, aged 41, or 38, labourer, Perthshire, 5'5" tall, dark hair, imprisoned in Lancaster Castle, transported 5 May 1747 from Liverpool to Antigua, Leeward Islands on *Veteran*, liberated by a French Privateer in Martinique Jun 1747, *P.3.244, PRO.SP36.102,ff.120r-121v*

ORR, DUNCAN, aged 14, born 1733, weaver, Perthshire, 4'8" tall, brown hair, sprightly transported 5 May 1747 from Liverpool to

the Leeward Islands on *Veteran*, liberated by a French Privateer in
Martinique Jun 1747, *P.3.244, PRO.SP36.102,ff.120r-121v*

OSWALD, JAMES, from Tullibardine, Lord John Drummond's
Regiment, imprisoned at Crieff, 2.5.1746 Perth, 12.5.1746 Stirling
Castle, Edinburgh, discharged 17.7.1747. "Gardener at
Tullibardine. Witnesses assert that he marched and did duty with
the rebel army, wore the White Cockade, and bore arms." *P.3.244*

PERTH, Dowager, Duchess of, JEAN, Drummond Castle, Perthshire,
imprisoned Feb 1746 Drummond Castle, 11.2.1746 Edinburgh
Castle, released 17.11.1746. "Subsists herself." Lady Jean
Gordon, daughter of George, 4th Marquis of Huntly, 1st Duke of
Gordon, married in 1706 James,fifth Earl and titular second Duke
of Perth. She was mother of the Duke of Perth of the '45 and of
Lord John Drummond. There is a discrepancy in regard to the
date of her being taken prisoner, as, according to the diary of James
Gib, the Prince's Master of the Household, she entertained the
Prince at Drummond Castle on 1 Feb 1746. She died at Stobhill,
30 Jan 1773 aged nearly 90 *P.3.250*

POOLEY, THOMAS, soldier in Roy Stewart's (Edinburgh) Regiment,
captured at the siege of Carlisle 30 Dec 1745 and imprisoned there.
No further reference to him *CA.3.132, P.3.254, MR.207*

POWRIE, JOHN or THOMAS, aged 17, shoemaker, Perth, imprisoned in
Carlisle and Lincoln Castle, died before 22.4.1747. "Went along
with the Rebels to England." *SHS.8.48, P.3.256*

PULLAR, JOHN, from Logiealmond, 3rd Battalion, Duke of Atholl's
Regiment, imprisoned 6.2.1746 Perth, discharged on bail 2.4.1746.
On suspicion. "For carrying treasonable letters from Edinburgh to
Perth." *P.3.258, MR.26*

RAMSAY, GEORGE, Ensign, Duke of Perth's Regiment, captured at
siege of Carlisle, 30 Dec 1745 *CA.3.131*

RAMSAY, PATRICK, Sketewan *CA.3.307*

RATTRAY, ANDREW, younger of Blackcraig, Ensign, Atholl Brigade,
CA.3.301, MR.21

RATTRAY, HENRY, from Alyth, Perthshire, Ogilvy's Regiment, imprisoned 30.12.1745 Carlisle Castle, York Castle. Was caputured at the surrender of Carlisle. There is no further reference to him, he may have died *P.3.264, SHS.8.232*

RATTRAY, JAMES, Major, of Corb, Kirkmichael, Perthshire, taken prisoner and carried to England *SHS.8.232*

RATTRAY, JAMES, aged 36, younger of Ranagulzion, Major, 3rd Battalion, Ogilvy's Regiment, taken prisoner Culloden, imprisoned 30.4.1746 Drimnie, 1.5.1746 Perth, Inverness, shipped on *HMS Winchilsea"* to London (Southwark), acquitted 2.9.1746. Son of David Rattray of Rannagulzion, he married the sister of Sir James Kinloch, Bt and served as major in Ogilvy's Regiment under Sir James. He was at Culloden and parted from the Prince at the Ford of Failie after the battle. He was captured by the Hessian cavalry at his house, together with Sir James and his brothers, Alexander and Charles Kinloch, and sent to London. At his trial in November 1746 he pleaded compulsion. This plea was rejected, until a witness swore that he had seen him handcuffed in the custody of the Prince's army. It appears that the Marquis of Tullibardine had claimed his services, as his vassal, for the Perthshire regiment. When he refused, as he preferred to serve in Ogilvy's, he was seized by order of the Marquis, and was only released when the true facts were made known to the latter. He was consequently acquitted and released by the Court without forfeiture. Nevertheless his property was wantonly damaged by the Government troops. *CA.3.301, P.3.264, MR.18*

RATTRAY, JAMES, brother to Tullochcurran, Ensign, Atholl Brigade, *CA.3.301, MR.21*

RATTRAY, JAMES, surgeon apprentice, Perth, volunteer, now lurking *SHS.8.50*

RATTRAY, JOHN, brother to Craighall, surgeon in Edinburgh, Surgeon in Prince's Army, taken prisoner Culloden, imprisoned 16.4.1746 Culloden, Inverness, 28.5.1746 Edinburgh, London (Messenger's house), liberated May 1746; again liberated 7.1.1747. Brother to James Rattray of Craighall. He was put in a church along with his friend Dr Lauder, among a crowd of prisoners; but their instruments were removed. He was captured on the field of Culloden while administering help. At Lord President Forbes' request to Cumberland he was released after a short detention. On arriving in Edinburgh he was again taken prisoner and sent to London, by Cumberland's orders, to act as witness. He was finally released 7 Jan 1747 *CA.3.301, P.3.264*

REID, ALEXANDER, Drumachaldane, Ensign, Atholl Brigade, *CA.3.301, MR.21*

REID, DAVID, in Conviallach, cottar, killed at Culloden, Atholl Brigade (paid listing money) *CA.3.304*

REID, DAVID, cottar, in Wester Kinnaird, Atholl Brigade, in south and in England *CA.3.304, MR.25*

REID, HUGH, Foss, brother to Alexander Reid of Drumachaldane, Ensign, Atholl Brigade, *CA.3.301, MR.21*

REID, JOHN, in Haugh of Tulliment, servant, Atholl Brigade (paid listing money), at Culloden *CA.3.303, MR.26*

REID, MALCOLM, in Cuilt of Balyoukan, servant, Atholl Brigade (paid listing money), at Culloden *CA.3.304, MR.26*

REID, PATRICK, in Ballinlochan, cottar, Atholl Brigade, in south and in England (paid listing money) *CA.3.304, MR.26*

REID, PATRICK, of Wester Kinnaird, cottar, Atholl Brigade, in south and in England, (paid listing money), killed *CA.3.304, MR.26*

REID, PETER, Merchant from Perth, imprisoned 7.2.1746 Perth, 1.4.1746 Edinburgh Castle, escaped 16 4.1746. Suspicion of treasonable practices. "Acted as Jailer under the rebels when they were in possession of Perth."*P.3.268*

REOCH, JOHN, cooper, Stanley, parish of Auchtergaven, Perthshire, carried arms as a volunteer during the whole rebellion *CA.3.306, SHS.8.232*

RIDDOCH, DUNCAN, servant, Tullibody, Gerrichrew, Perthshire, Duke of Perth's Regiment, imprisoned Bagonie, Stirling 1.2.1746, 7.2.1747 Stirling Castle, 13.2.1746 Leith, 25.6.146 Edinburgh Jail, discharged 25.3.1747. Servant to William Forrester, Tullibody.

Taken in arms. "Denies that he was concerned with the rebels or carried arms with them." *P.3.272, MR.75*

RIDDOCH, JAMES, Drummond, Muthill, volunteer, now at home *SHS.8.50*

ROBERTSON, ...?, brother to Trinafour, Officer, Atholl Brigade, killed Culloden, (auth. Garth's list) *CA.3.298, CA.3.301, MR.21*

ROBERTSON, ...?, brother to Donald Robertson of Woodsheel, officer, now lurking *SHS.8.48*

ROBERTSON, Hon Mrs, of Lude, sister to Lord Nairne, 1st cousin to Duke, active in raising men, her son a minor *CA.3.301*

ROBERTSON, ALEXANDER, Major General, of Struan, Atholl Brigade, escaped *SHS.8.48, MR.18*

ROBERTSON, ALEXANDER, (1689, 1715), of Struan, too old for service, sent his men, present at Prestonpans; returned to Rannoch in General Cope's carriage *CA.3.301*
Alexander Robertson succeeded to the estate in 1688, was involved in the Jacobite risings in 1689 and 1715, was eventually pardoned, and lived upon the estate for several years before 1745. Though then an old man, he gave all the countenance and aid in his power to the cause of the Pretender, for which he was attainted, and his estates forfeited. He died in his own house of Carie in 1749, in the 81st year of his age, leaving a volume of poems in manuscript which was afterwards published *SHS.8.372*

ROBERTSON, ALEXANDER, son of Inverack, brother to Woodshiel (rank unknown), killed *CA.3.298*

ROBERTSON, ALEXANDER, son of Robert Robertson of Bohespick, Ensign, Atholl Brigade *CA.3.301, MR.21*

ROBERTSON, ALEXANDER, son of Donald Robertson of Woodshiel, Officer, Atholl Brigade, killed Culloden *CA.3.301, MR.20*

ROBERTSON, ALEXANDER, Wadsetter of Clunes, Ensign, Atholl Brigade *CA.3.301, MR.21*

ROBERTSON, ALEXANDER, dyer, Bridge End of Gilt, 3rd Battalion, Atholl Brigade, taken prisoner, turned King's Evidence and was discharged *MR.26*

ROBERTSON, ALEXANDER, of Raimore, Ensign, lived at Guay, parish of Douly, Atholl Brigade, joined as a volunteer and continued to their dispersion, lurking *CA.3.301, MR.21, SHS.8.232*

ROBERTSON, ALEXANDER, in Ballnacree, Atholl Brigade, in south and in England *CA.3.304, MR.26*

ROBERTSON, ALEXANDER, in Dunchastle, Atholl Brigade, (paid listing money), killed at Culloden *CA.3.304, MR.25*

ROBERTSON, ALEXANDER, West Craggan *CA.3.307*

ROBERTSON, ALEXANDER, born 1707, tenant or labourer in Struan, 3rd Battalion, Atholl Brigade, taken prisoner November 1745, transported 5 May 1747 from Liverpool to the Leeward Islands on *Veteran*, liberated by a French Privateer in Martinique Jun 1747, *P.3.276, MR.26, PRO.SP36.102*

ROBERTSON, ALEXANDER, Sheriff Officer, Perth, imprisoned 10.2.1746 Perth, 30.3.1746 Edinburgh, liberated 15.7.1747. Treasonable practices. "Ran errands for the rebels and went at their desire to warn in carts and horses from the country to carry their baggage." *P.3.276*

ROBERTSON, ANGUS, Stratherrol, 3rd Battalion, Duke of Atholl's Regiment, imprisoned 6.7.1746 Stratherrol, 6.7.1746 Dundee, discharged 16.3.1747 *P.3.276, MR.26*

ROBERTSON, CHARLES, son of Invervack, brother of Woodshiel, died of wounds (rank unknown), killed *CA.3.298*

ROBERTSON, CHARLES, Lieutenant, younger of Balnacree, Atholl Brigade, son of James Robertson of Balnacree, killed at Culloden *CA.3.298, CA.3.301, CA.3.304, CA.3.308, MR.20*

ROBERTSON, CHARLES, younger of Trinafour, Officer, Atholl Brigade, *CA.3.301, MR.20*

ROBERTSON, CHARLES, son of Donald Robertson of Woodshiel, Officer, Atholl Brigade, killed (died of wounds) Culloden *CA.3.301, MR.21*

ROBERTSON, CHARLES, younger of Balnaguard, Officer, Atholl Brigade, *CA.3.301, CA.3.308, MR.20*

ROBERTSON, CHARLES, farmer, Raimore, Caputh, Perthshire, "joined the rebels as a volunteer before the battle of Falkirk," lurking *CA.3.306, SHS.8.232*

ROBERTSON, CHARLES, Guay *CA.3.307*

ROBERTSON, CHARLES, merchant apprentice, Eastertyoungere, Little Dunkeld, acted as an officer, now lurking *SHS.8.48*

ROBERTSON, CHARLES, soldier in Roy Stewart's Regiment, captured at the siege of Carlisle 30 Dec 1745, *CA.3.132*

ROBERTSON, CHARLES, from Runroy, Lude, Atholl, in 3rd Battalion, Tullibardine's Regiment (Duke of Atholl), imprisoned 3.8.1746 Perth, turned King's Evidence, and discharged 25.7.1747. This man gave evidence against Lady Lude and stated he had been forced out *P.3.276, MR.26*

ROBERTSON, CHARLOTTE, Lady Lude *CA.3.308*

ROBERTSON, DANIEL, Blair Atholl *CA.3.306*

ROBERTSON, DANIEL, from Glenshee, "in rebel service", imprisoned Argyllshire, 31.5.1746 Perth, Stirling, 8.8.1746 Carlisle. There is no further reference to him *P.3.176*

ROBERTSON, DANIEL, aged 28 from Perthshire, Lord George Murray's Regiment, 2nd Battalion, (Duke of Atholl), imprisoned Inverness June 1746, shipped on *Wallsgrave* to Tilbury. There is no further reference to him *P.3.176, MR.26*

ROBERTSON, DAVID, Captain, of Easter Bleaton, Alyth, parish of Kirkmichael, Perthshire, Tullibardine's Regiment (Duke of Atholl's), imprisoned 27.1.1747 Blaiton, 24.1.1747 Dundee, discharged 16.3.1747. "Gentleman." "In the rebellion." His name appeared in the list of persons excepted from the general Act of Pardon, "has been at home" *P.3.278, CA.3.301, CA.3.308, MR.19, SHS.8.232*

ROBERTSON, DONALD, Captain, of Woodshiel, Fortingall, Struan
Robertson's Regiment, commanding Struan's men, wounded at
Culloden, imprisoned 10.8.1746 in Canongate, released under
General Pardon, 1747 *CA.3.298, SHS.8.48, P.3.278, MR.18*

ROBERTSON, DONALD, cousin to Woodshiel, with Struan's men?
(rank unknown) wounded *CA.3.298*

ROBERTSON, DONALD, of Woodshiel, son of Robert Robertson of
Wester Invervack, Commanded Struan's men, wounded Culloden
CA.3.301

ROBERTSON, DONALD, nephew of Donald Robertson of Woodshiel,
Officer, Atholl Brigade, wounded Culloden *CA.3.301, MR.21*

ROBERTSON, DONALD, in Craig'nuisk, tenant, Atholl Brigade, in
south and in England *CA.3.303, MR.26*

ROBERTSON, DONALD, cottar, Tullimet, Atholl Brigade (paid listing
money), killed at Culloden *CA.3.303, MR.26*

ROBERTSON, DONALD, in Cruishill, Atholl Brigade (paid listing
money), wounded at Culloden *CA.3.303, MR.26*

ROBERTSON, DONALD, in Dunfalandy, Atholl Brigade, (paid listing
money) killed at Culloden *CA.3.305, MR.26*

ROBERTSON, DONALD, West Craggan *CA.3.307*

ROBERTSON, DONALD, Logierait, Chapman *CA.3.307*

ROBERTSON, DONALD, younger of Kincragie *CA.3.308*

ROBERTSON, DUNCAN, Captain, of Auchleeks or Auchlecke, Atholl
Brigade, wounded, Culloden *CA.3.298, CA.3.301, CA.3.308,
MR.19*

ROBERTSON, DUNCAN, of Calvine, Officer, Atholl Brigade, killed
Culloden, (auth. Garth's list) was also tenant at Dalnamein,
CA.3.298, CA.3.301, MR.21

ROBERTSON, DUNCAN, of Dalnamein, *CA.3.301*

ROBERTSON, DUNCAN, Colonel, Atholl Brigade, of Drumachine,
parish of Foss, No 4 Battalion, escaped abroad *CA.3.301,
SHS.8.48, MR.18*

ROBERTSON, FINLAY, in Ballnakeilly's ground, Atholl Brigade (paid
listing money), in south and in England *CA.3.305, MR.27*

ROBERTSON, GEORGE, of Faskally, Lieutenant Colonel 3rd Battalion,
seduced by the Marquis of Tullibardine, whereabouts not known
CA.3.301, SHS.8.48, MR.18
On the retreat of the rebel army from Stirling northwards, in
February 1746, they were reinforced at Perth by this laird. The
Scots Magazine reports that on 2 February "there came in from
Crief 140 men, commanded by Mr Robertson of Fascally and Mr
James Robertson of Blairfetty, and brought in seven pieces of brass
cannon and four convered waggons." They crossed the Tay on 4th
of the same month, on the way northwards. *SHS.8.372*

ROBERTSON, GEORGE, in Badvo, Atholl Brigade, killed at Culloden
CA.3.304, MR.27

ROBERTSON, GEORGE, aged 21, born 1726, apprentice to a weaver of
Logginish or Logierait, Lord George Murray's Regiment, 2nd
Battalion, Atholl Brigade, imprisoned Inverness and taken south in
May 1746 on board *Jane of Leith* to Tilbury Fort. Transported 31
March 1747 from London to Barbados on *Frere, P.3.278, MR.27,
CA.3.316*

ROBERTSON, GEORGE, Rev, Edreedynot, Perthshire, imprisoned in
Perth, released. Non-Jurant episcopal minister, brought before
sherrifs by Lieutenant Courtney "for praying publicly in his
meeting house for the Pretender.... Committed to Tolbooth. As
yet no proof brought against him." *P.3.278*

ROBERTSON, GILBERT, in Dunfalandy, Atholl Brigade, at Culloden
CA.3.305, MR.27

ROBERTSON, JAMES, Captain, of Balnacree, Atholl Brigade, killed,
Culloden, *CA.3.298, CA.3.301, CA.3.304, CA.3.308, MR.19*

ROBERTSON, JAMES (1715), of Blairfettie, Major, 2nd Battalion Atholl Brigade, *CA.3.301, CA.3.308, MR.18*
On the retreat of the rebel army from Stirling northwards, in February 1746, they were reinforced at Perth by this laird. The *Scots Magazine* reports that on 2 February "there came in from Crief 140 men, commanded by Mr Robertson of Fascally and Mr James Robertson of Blairfetty, and brought in seven pieces of brass cannon and four convered waggons." They crossed the Tay on 4th of the same month, on the way northwards. *SHS.8.372*

ROBERTSON, JAMES, Col, of Blairfetty, parish of Blair, very active in pressing men into service, now lurking *SHS.8.48*

ROBERTSON, JAMES, nephew of Donald Robertson of Woodshiel, Officer, Atholl Brigade, killed in Fealar whilst skulking after Culloden *CA.3.301, MR.21*

ROBERTSON, JAMES, Captain, of Killiechangie, Logierait, Captain Struan's man, died at Moness 1820, aged 95; the last of the Atholl officers who served in the '45, deserted Atholl Brigade before the Battle of Falkirk, now at home, *SHS.8.48, CA.3.301, CA.3.308, MR.19*

ROBERTSON, JAMES, younger of Killiechangie, aged 20, Officer, Atholl Brigade, pardoned *CA.3.301, SHS.8.48, MR.21*

ROBERTSON, JAMES, in Countlich, cottar, Atholl Brigade, (paid listing money), at Culloden *CA.3.303, MR.27*

ROBERTSON, JAMES, in Ballachragan, cottar, killed at Culloden, Atholl Brigade (paid listing money) *CA.3.304, MR.27*

ROBERTSON, JAMES, Captain, of Killiechangie, vassal to Strowan, served in his regiment, officer, in south and in England *CA.3.305*

ROBERTSON, JAMES, Lieutenant, son of Captain James Robertson of Killiechangie, officer, at Culloden *CA.3.305*

ROBERTSON, JAMES, groom to Lord George Murray *CA.3.306*

ROBERTSON, JOHN, Quartermaster, of Wester Bohespick, killed Culloden *CA.3.298, CA.3.301, CA.3.308, MR.22*

ROBERTSON, JOHN, nephew of Donald Robertson of Woodshiel, Quartermaster, left at home in charge of a party *CA.3.301, MR.22*

ROBERTSON, JOHN, younger of Kincraigie, Officer, Atholl Brigade, *CA.3.301, MR.21*

ROBERTSON, JOHN, tenant of Killichangie, Atholl Brigade *MR.27*

ROBERTSON, JOHN, younger of Eastertyoungere, Officer, Atholl Brigade, *CA.3.301, MR.21*

ROBERTSON, JOHN, son of late Guay, Officer, Atholl Brigade, *CA.3.301, MR.21*

ROBERTSON, JOHN, in Achnabechan, Atholl Brigade, at Culloden *CA.3.303, MR.27*

ROBERTSON, JOHN, in Blairchroisk, Atholl Brigade, at Culloden (paid listing money) *CA.3.304, MR.27*

ROBERTSON, JOHN, in Badvo, Atholl Brigade, at Culloden (paid listing money) *CA.3.304, MR.27*

ROBERTSON, JOHN, in Ballintuim, Atholl Brigade, in south and in England *CA.3.305, MR.27*

ROBERTSON, JOHN, tenant to Captain James Robertson of Killiechangie, at Culloden *CA.3.305*

ROBERTSON, JOHN, from Stratherrol, Captain Ogilvy's Regiment, imprisoned 6.7.1746 Stratherrol, 6.7.1746 Dundee, 8.8.1746 Carlisle, Chester, transported 1747, *P.3.278, MR.91*

ROBERTSON, LAURENCE, mason, Dunkeld, went in arms with the rebels on their retreat north, whereabouts not known *CA.3.306, SHS.8.50*

ROBERTSON, NEIL, cordwainer, Logierait, soldier of Lord George Murray's Regiment, 2nd Battalion, Atholl Brigade, captured at siege of Carlisle, 30 Dec 1745, imprisoned in Carlisle and Chester Castle, transported 22 Apr 1747 from Liverpool to Virginia on *Johnson*, landed at Port Oxford, Maryland, 5 Aug 1747 *P.3.278, MR.27, PRO.T1.328, CA3.132*

ROBERTSON, PATRICK, of Trinafour, Captain, Atholl Brigade, Commanding at Dalnacardoch *CA.3.301, MR.19*

ROBERTSON, ROBERT (ban) (1715), of Wester Invervack, Officer, Atholl Brigade, commanded Struan's escort on his return home *CA.3.301, MR.21*

ROBERTSON, THOMAS, Captain, farmer, Windyedge, parish of Aberdagie, Perthshire, imprisoned in Canongate and Carlisle (or still lurking). A "journeyman" goldsmith in Edinburgh" of this name appears in the list of men sent to Carlisle. It may have been this man. A man of this name, aged 20, a barber, appears in the Carlisle list for transportation. It appears unlikely that he would have been a Captain at that age. *CA.3.301, SHS.8.50, P.3.280, MR.19*

ROBERTSON, WILLIAM, aged 17, born 1730, labourer, Perthshire, 5'5" tall, brown hair, well made, Duke of Perth's Regiment, taken after the siege of Carlisle and imprisoned 30.12.1745 Carlisle, and York Castle. Transported 8 May 1747 from Liverpool to Antigua, Leeward Islands on *Veteran*, liberated by a French Privateer in Martinique Jun 1747, *P.3.280, MR.75, PRO.SP36.102,ff.120r-121v*

ROBERTSON, WILLIAM, Perthshire, 3rd Battalion, Atholl Brigade, (deserter from Guise's), taken prisoner at Culloden, hanged *MR.27*

ROBERTSON, WILLIAM GILBERT, Glentilt, Atholl Brigade, pardoned *MR.27*

ROBINSON, ALEXANDER, aged 40, labourer, Perthshire, 5'2" tall, dark hair, pale, transported 5 May 1747 from Liverpool to the Leeward Islands on *Veteran*, liberated by a French Privateer in Martinique Jun 1747, *P.3.276, MR.26, PRO.SP36.102,ff.120r-121v*

ROBINSON, CHARLES, aged 40, labourer of Dullater, Perthsire, Roy Stuart's (Edinburgh) Regiment, imprisoned 30.12.1745 Carlisle, Chester Castle, Lancaster Castle and York. Pardoned on condition of enlistment 22.7.1748. Taken at capture of Carlisle. Was tried at York, October 1746 and sentenced to death, but reprieved and pardoned on enlistment *P.3.282, MR.207*

ROBINSON, GEORGE, aged 20 from Perthshire, Lord George Murray's Regiment, 2nd Battalion, Atholl Brigade, imprisoned Inverness June 1746, shipped on the *Wallsgrave*. No further reference to him, probably died *P.3.282, MR.27*

ROBINSON, JOHN, labourer from Pitleoch, Perthshire, Lord George Murray's Regiment, imprisoned in Carlisle and Chester. There is no further reference to him *P.3.282*

ROSE, ALEXANDER, aged 18, 2nd Battalion, Atholl Brigade, taken prisoner, transported 1 Mar 1747from London to Barbados, in *Frere P.3.284, MR.128, MR.27*

ROSE, ALEXANDER, aged 29, servant to Gordon of Carroll, 2nd Battalion, Atholl Brigade, taken prisoner, transported *MR.27*

ROY, DUNCAN, Drummond, Muthill, volunteer, now at home *SHS.8.50*

SANDERS, GEORGE, in Riechip, cottarman, Atholl Brigade, in south and in England, killed *CA.3.303, MR.27*

SANGSTER, JOHN, Stanley, parish of Auchtergaven, late servant to Lord Nairne, 1st Battalion, Atholl Brigade, was a volunteer and carried arms, whereabouts not known *CA.3.306, MR.27, SHS.8.236*

SCOTT, ALEXANDER, soldier in Roy Stewart's (Appin's?) Regiment, captured at the siege of Carlisle 30 Dec 1745 imprisoned in Carlisle and York Castle, pardoned on condition of enlistment 22.7.1748. Was tried Oct 1746 and was sentenced to death, but reprieved *CA.3.132, P.3.300*

SCOTT, GEORGE, Captain, son of James Scott, Vintner, Dunkeld, Atholl Brigade, killed Culloden *CA.3.298, CA.3.301, MR.19*

SCOTT, JAMES, Vintner, Dunkeld, not out; taken prisoner Feb 1746 *CA.3.301*

SCOTT, JAMES, workman, Dunkeld, Ogilvy's Regiment, imprisoned 6.5.1746 Dundee, 6.5.1746 Montrose, 9.8.1746 Edinburgh *CA.3.306, SHS.8.52, P.3.302*

SCOTT, JOHN, mason, Dunkeld, surrendered *CA.3.306, SHS.8.52*

SCOTT, JOHN, aged 17, born 1730, herd, Perthshire, 5'4" tall, light hair, fair faced, slender, soldier in Roy Stewart's Regiment, captured at the siege of Carlisle 30 Dec 1745, transported 5 May 1747 from Liverpool to the Leeward Islands on *Veteran*, liberated by a French Privateer in Martinique Jun 1747, *MR.209, CA.3.132, PRO.SP36.102,ff.120r-121v*

SCOTT, JOHN, aged 17, Herd from Atholl, Roy Stuart's Regiment, imprisoned 30.12.1745 Carlisle and York Castle, pardoned on condition of enlistment 22.7.1748. Taken at capture of Carlisle *P.3.302, MR.207*

SCOTT, WILLIAM, Perthshire, soldier in Roy Stewart's Regiment, captured at the siege of Carlisle 30 Dec 1745, imprisoned in Carlisle and York Castle, pardoned on condition of enlistment 22.7.1748. He was tried at York 2 Oct 1746, found guilty and sentenced to death, but reprieved and pardoned on enlistment, *CA.3.132, P.3.304, MR.207*

SEATON, ANDREW, Chapman, Alyth, Perthshire, carried arms in Lord Ogilvie's 1st Battalion, come home *SHS.8.236*

SHAW, MARGARET, aged 15, spinner from Perthshire, imprisoned in Carlisle and Lancaster Castle, transported 22 Apr 1747 from Liverpool to Virginia in *Johnson*, arrived Port Oxford, Maryland 5 Aug 1747 *P.3.308, PRO.T1.328*

SHEPHERD, CHARLES, shoemaker, Minfield, parish of Forgan, Perthshire, was a soldier in Lord Ogilvie's 2nd Battalion, returned home *SHS.8.236*

SHOWER, EDWARD, Captain Artillery, imprisoned in Perth 10.3.1746, died 9.3.1746?? "An English papist, confessed he was present in the rebell's trenches while they were firing their cannon at Stirling Castle." *P.3.312*

SHOWSTER, JOHN, resident of Scone, concerned in a mob and in arms at Perth on the anniversary of His Majesty's Birthday, went north with the rebels *SHS.8.50*

SIMM, JOHN, aged 18 from Perthshire, Lord Nairn's Regiment, Atholl Brigade, imprisoned Inverness June 1746, shipped on south on *Thane of Fife*. No further reference to him *P.3.312*

SINCLAIR, AENEAS, Comrie, pressed by the rebels into their service, now at home *SHS.8.50*

SINCLAIR, DUNCAN, Innerhadden *CA.3.307*

SMITH, JAMES, Perth, Surgeon, imprisoned 7.2.1746 Perth, 1.4.1746 Edinburgh Jail from Castle, liberated 20.6.1746. On suspicion of treason *P.3.322*

SMITH, JAMES, Perthshire, Struan Robertson's Regiment, Atholl Brigade, deserted/imprisoned 4.11.1745 Pentland Hills, Edinburgh Castle, 15.1.1746 Edinburgh Jail, discharged *P.3.322, MR.27*

SMITH, JOHN, from Bahallarie, Alyth, Perthshire, imprisoned 26.5.1746 Bahallarie, 26.5.1746 Dundee, discharged 16.3.1747. "Was active in serving the rebels." *P.3.324, SHS.8.236*

SMITH, WILLIAM, resident of Drummond, parish of Muthill, volunteer, now at home *SHS.8.50*

SOMERVELL, DAVID, Lord John Drummond's Regiment, died Perth, 15.8.1746 *P.1.188*

SPALDING, ANDREW, Lieutenant Colonel, of Glenkilrie, Atholl Brigade, *CA.3.301, MR.18*

SPALDING, CHARLES, Captain, of Whitfield, 3rd Battalion, Atholl Brigade, taken prisoner, Kilsyth Nov 1745, pardoned *CA.3.301, MR.19*

SPALDING, DANIEL (or DAVID), Captain, of Ashintuillie, Atholl Brigade, *CA.3.301, MR.19*

SPALDING, DANIEL (or DAVID) Captain, natural son of Daniel Spalding of Ashintuillie, Atholl Brigade, *CA.3.301, MR.19*

SPALDING, JOHN, younger of Whitfield, Officer, Atholl Brigade *CA.3.301, MR.21, MR.27*

SPALDING, JOHN, younger of Glenkilrie, Officer, Atholl Brigade *MR.21*

SPALDING, JOHN, Ennod, Strathardle, 3rd Battalion (Capt Murray's) Atholl Brigade, pardoned *MR.27*

STALKER, JOHN, Condie Cleuch, parish of Monzie, carried arms as a private man in rebel service, but pressed out, now at home *SHS.8.50*

STALKER, PETER, servant to John Stalker, Glenlednek, parish of Comrie, pressed by the rebels into their service, now at home *SHS.8.50*

STEEL, MICHAEL, labourer from Logiealmond, Pertshire, Duke of Atholl's Regiment, imprisoned 3.6.1746 Perth, 10.8.1746 Canongate, Carlisle. Transported 22 Apr 1747 from Liverpool to Virginia, in *Johnson*, arrived Port North Potomac, Maryland, 5 Aug 1747 *P.3.322, MR.27, PRO.T1.328*

STEWART, ...?, brother of William Stewart of Garth, Officer, Atholl Brigade, *CA.3.302, MR.21*

STEWART, ...?, brother to Tullochroisk, officer, killed Culloden *CA.3.302*

STEWART, ...?, weaver, Balmaniel, parish of Logierait, was an officer, is sometimes at home, but lurking *SHS.8.50*

STEWART, ALAN, Captain, of Innerhadden, Captain of Grandtully's men, Roy Stewart's Regiment *CA.3.302*

STEWART, ALEXANDER, Ensign, in Ardgie, wounded *CA.3.298*

STEWART, ALEXANDER, of Duntanlich, Officer, Atholl Brigade, *CA.3.302, MR.21*

STEWART, ALEXANDER, Ensign, son of William Stewart of Ardgie, wounded Culloden *CA.3.302, MR.22*

STEWART, ALEXANDER, brother of John Stewart of Findynate, (late of Loudon's), Officer, Atholl Brigade *CA.3.302, MR.21*

STEWART, ALEXANDER, of Glen Buckie, Balquhidder, Duke of Perth's Regiment. In September 1745 on his march to join the

Prince, Glen Buckie slept at Leny and was found shot dead in his bed; supposed suicide *CA.3.302*

STEWART, ALEXANDER, Ensign, in Ardgie, wounded, at Culloden *CA.3.304*

STEWART, ALEXANDER, in Ballnakeily's ground, Atholl Brigade (paid listing money), at Culloden *CA.3.305, MR.27*

STEWART, ALEXANDER, in Middle Dalguise, servant Atholl Brigade (paid listing money), in south and in England *CA.3.305, MR.27*

STEWART, ALEXANDER, Sheriff Officer, Perth, together with Finlay Stewart, employed as spy by Lord Strathallan, active in oppressing the country and charging people to pay revenue to rebels, imprisoned 12.2.1746 Perth, 1.4.1746 Edinburgh Jail, released under General Pardon, 1747. *SHS.8.50, P.3.334*

STEWART, ALEXANDER, Meikleour, 3rd Battalion, Atholl Brigade, pardoned *MR.27*

STEWART, ALEXANDER, aged 34, born 1713, footman to the Prince, and said to have been servant to Mrs Murray of Broughton. An account of his imprisonment, treatment, and ultimate transportation appeared in Bishop Forbes' *Lyon*. He was one of the few who escaped from America and got back to Scotland in 1748. Imprisoned 29.4.1746 Rannegoolen, Perth, 9.8.1746 Falkland, 10.8.1746 Canongate, 12.8.1746 Carlisle, 24.4.1747 Penrith, 25.4.1747 Kendal, 27.4.1747 Lancaster, 28.4.1747 Preston, 30.4.1747 Liverpool, transported 14 May 1747 on *Gildart* from Liverpool to Wicomica, Maryland, arrived at Port North Potomac, Maryland 5 Aug 1747, *P.3.336, MR.8, PRO.T1.328*

STEWART, ALLAN, aged 33, ale seller near Doune, Perthshire, Stewart of Ardshiel's Regiment (Appin's), imprisoned in Inverness June 1746, shipped on *Wallsgrave* to Tilbury Fort. "A notorious Jacobite." No further reference to him, he may have died. *P.3.336*

STEWART, ANDREW, Perth, imprisoned in Perth, discharged on bail 29.3.1746 *P.3.336*

STEWART, CHARLES, Adjutant, of Bohally, parish of Weem, No 1 Battalion, Atholl Brigade, (later of Appin's), had command of his own tenants, wounded Culloden when with Appin's Regiment, lurking in hills *CA.2.298, CA.3.302, CA.3.308, SHS.8.50, MR.19*

STEWART, CHARLES, Captain, of Balechin, Atholl Brigade, pardoned *CA.3.302, MR.19*

STEWART, CHARLES, Lieutenant Colonel, jr. of Ballachan, Logierait, now lurking in the hills *SHS.8.50*

STEWART, CHARLES, Captain, of Wester Gourdie, parish of Caputh, Atholl Brigade during the whole rebellion, whereabouts not known *CA.3.302, MR.19, SHS.8.236*

STEWART, CHARLES, Adjutant, Atholl Brigade, cousin of Patrick Stewart of Easter Invervack *CA.3.302, MR.19*

STEWART, DANIEL, from Perth, Roy Stuart's (Edinburgh) Regiment, taken at capture of Carlisle, imprisoned 30.12.1745 Carlisle. No further reference to him *P.3.338, MR.207*

STEWART, DANIEL, farmer from Drumoar, Perthshire, Royal Stuart's (Edinburgh) Regiment, taken at capture of Carlisle, imprisoned Carlisle 30.12.1745 and Chester Castle. No further reference to him *P.3.338, MR.207*

STEWART, DAVID, Captain, of Balvorest, Atholl Brigade *MR.19*

STEWART, DAVID, Major, of Kynachan, parish of Foss, 1st Battalion, Atholl Brigade, killed Culloden, (or lurking in hills) *CA.3.298, CA.3.302, CA.3.308, SHS.8.50, MR.21*

STEWART, DAVID, Major, of Ballahallan, parish of Callander, Lord George Murray's Regiment, Brother of Stewart of Ardvorlich. "Collected his Majesty's Revenue". He was caught with six other refugees in a hut on the Braes of Leny. He put up a stiff fight, but was taken to Stirling, where he died of his wounds. The Prisoner's Roll shows that while in prison he was in hospital with a gunshot wound of the thigh, and that a surgeon's fee of 6s.8d. was paid for treating him. The evidence brought against him was that "he was seen at Dunblane dressed and armed like a rebel Highlander wearing a white Cockade. Others stated that he acted as rebel officer in taking possession of Castle Doune with a body of armed men." He was specially excepted from the Act of pardon of June

1747. Collected his Majesty's Revenue for the rebels. Imprisoned 19.7.1746 Braes of Leny, 20.7.1746 Stirling Castle *SHS.8.60, P.3.338, MR.18*

STEWART, DONALD (or DANIEL), of Strathgarry, soldier in Roy Stewart's Regiment, captured at the siege of Carlisle 30 Dec 1745, *CA.3.132, CA.3.302*

STEWART, DONALD, of Dalvorest *CA.3.302*

STEWART, DONALD, in Reichip, Caputh parish, not a tenant, son to Strathgairie, a schoolboy, Atholl Brigade, carried arms from a little before the battle of Falkirk, seduced by Glenbucket, in south and in England, whereabouts not known *CA.3.303, MR.28, SHS.8.236*

STEWART, DONALD, servant to John Inches in Leducky, killed, in south and in England *CA.3.303*

STEWART, DONALD, Drum of Pitlochry, Atholl Brigade, in south and in England (paid listing money) *CA.3.304, MR.28*

STEWART, DONALD, Middle Dalguise, Atholl Brigade, in south and in England *CA.3.305, MR.28*

STEWART, DUNCAN, born 1726, cattleherd in Breadalbane, soldier in Roy Stewart's (Edinburgh) Regiment, captured at the siege of Carlisle 30 Dec 1745, transported 1747 *P.3.340, CA.3.132, MR.207*

STEWART, DUNCAN, tailor of Strathbrand, Dunkeld, Roy Stuart's Regiment, captured at surrender of Carlisle. Imprisoned 30.12.1745 Carlisle and York, pardoned on condition of enlistment 22.7.1748. At his trial at York, 2 Oct 1746, evidence was brought that the district in which he lived could have produced 350 men but only one man came out, that 100 Frasers came down and forced the inhabitants out, and that he was one of them who was taken to Edinburgh. The all deserted, but he did not; and although once he tried to desert at Ashbourne he was subsequently seen in arms at Carlisle. He was sentenced to death but reprieved and pardoned on enlistment *P.3.342, MR.207*

STEWART, FINLAY, Sheriff Officer, Perth, imprisoned 10.2.1746 Perth, 1.4.1746 Edinburgh Jail, released under General Pardon, 1747. Suspicion of treasonable practices. In hospital, 30.6.1746 with ague and "great cough." "Employed (with Alexander Stuart, Sheriff Officer) as spies by Lord Strathallan; were active in oppressing the country and charging the people to pay the revenue to the rebels *SHS.8.50, P.3.342*

STEWART, GILBERT, Captain, younger of Wester Kinnaird, Atholl Brigade, died of wounds, at Culloden *CA.3.298, CA.3.302, CA.3.304, CA.3.308, MR.19*

STEWART, HENRY, Captain, of Fincastle, Atholl Brigade *CA.3.302, CA.3.308, MR.19*

STEWART, HUGH, Temper *CA.3.307*

STEWART, JAMES, younger of Inch Garth (rank unknown), killed Culloden, *CA.3.298, CA.3.302, CA.3.308*

STEWART, JAMES, of Laigh of Cluny, Officer, Atholl Brigade, killed at Culloden *CA.3.298, CA.3.302, MR.21*

STEWART, JAMES, Lieutenant, brother to Tullochchroisk, Atholl Brigade, killed at Culloden (auth Garth's list) *CA.3.298, MR.20*

STEWART, JAMES, of Pitdornie, wadsetter, Officer, Atholl Brigade, *CA.3.302, CA.3.308*

STEWART, JAMES, Lieutenant, younger of Tullochcroisk, Atholl Brigade, *CA.3.302, MR.20*

STEWART, JAMES, Captain, son of James Stewart in Clunes, Atholl Brigade, *CA.3.302, MR.19*

STEWART, JAMES, younger of Inchgarth, Officer, Atholl Brigade, killed Culloden *CA.3.303, MR.21*

STEWART, JAMES, Captain, from Clunes, Atholl Brigade, wounded, Culloden, broke his arm by a fall at Ecclefechan on the march south, was left there sick, and rejoined when the Prince retreated into Scotland *CA.3.298, CA.3.302, CA.3.303, MR.19*

STEWART, JAMES, Lieutenant, of Wester Kinnaird, at Culloden *CA.3.304*

STEWART, JAMES, Drum of Pitlochry, Atholl Brigade, (paid listing money), in south and in England *CA.3.304, MR.28*

STEWART, JAMES, Middle Dalguise, servant, Atholl Brigade, in south and in England *CA.3.305, MR.28*

STEWART, JAMES, tobacconist, Dunkeld, absconding *CA.3.306, SHS.8.52*

STEWART, JAMES, resident of Cannband, Comrie, carried arms but forced out, now at home *SHS.8.50*

STEWART, JAMES, Drummond, parish of Muthill, volunteer, whereabouts not known *SHS.8.52*

STEWART, JAMES, tenant in Glengorlundy, Perthshire, 3rd Battalion, Duke of Atholl's Regiment, deserted. Imprisoned 20.2.1746 at home, Perth, 1.4.1746 Edinburgh Jail; released under General Pardon, 1747. On suspicion of treasonable practices. Says he "carried arms for 2 days," also that "he was seized in his own house by a party of rebel McPhersons and carried by them towards Crieff, where he deserted them." *P.3.344, MR.28*

STEWART, JAMES, Gentleman to Perth, taken prisoner, pardoned *MR.67*

STEWART, JOHN, nephew of Neil Stewart of Temper, Officer, Atholl Brigade, *CA.3.302, MR.21*

STEWART, JOHN, second son of Foss, Officer Atholl Brigade, *CA.3.302, MR.21*

STEWART, JOHN, of Pitaneasie, Officer, Atholl Brigade, *CA.3.302, MR.21*

STEWART, JOHN, Lieutenant, of Croftmore, Atholl Brigade, *CA.3.302, CA.3.308, MR.20*

STEWART, JOHN, of Findynate, parish of Logierait, he and his brother, Alexander, had both enlisted as privates in Captain Murray's Company of Loudoun's Highlanders, 1745, now lurking *CA.3.302, CA.3.308, SHS.8.50, MR.21*

STEWART, JOHN, (1715), Captain, brother to Easter Kinnaird, Atholl Brigade, was reported to have deserted from the Prince's army during the march north, February 1746 *CA.3.302, CA.3.308, MR.19*

STEWART, JOHN, younger of Stenton, Officer, parish of Caputh, Perthshire, Atholl Brigade, carried arms from a little before battle of Falkirk, left them on their return from Falkirk, seduced by Glenbucket to leave the school, "now in the country," afterwards served as a Captain in the 42nd Highlanders, 1758-71 *CA.3.302, MR.21, SHS.8.236*

STEWART, JOHN, Lieutenant, of Ledereich, Balquhidder, Duke of Perth's *CA.3.302, CA.3.308, MR.68*

STEWART, JOHN, a weaver lad in Little Dunkeld, Atholl Brigade, in south and in England, killed *CA.3.303, MR.28*

STEWART, JOHN, in Badvo, killed at Culloden Atholl Brigade, (paid listing money) *CA.3.304, MR.28*

STEWART, JOHN, in Ballaghulan, killed, at Culloden *CA.3.304*

STEWART, JOHN, in Middle Dalguise, Atholl Brigade, in south and in England *CA.3.305, MR.28*

STEWART, JOHN, Captain, in Kinnaird, officer, in south and in England *CA.3.305*

STEWART, JOHN, Drumnacreich *CA.3.306*

STEWART, JOHN, Invertilt *CA.3.307*

STEWART, JOHN, merchant apprentice in Perth, volunteer, now lurking *SHS.8.50*

STEWART, JOHN, aged 18, labourer, Perthshire, 5'4" tall, dark hair, lively, soldier in Roy Stewart's (Edinburgh) Regiment, captured at the siege of Carlisle 30 Dec 1745, imprisoned in Carlisle and York Castle, transported 8 May 1747 from Liverpool to Antigua, Leeward Islands on *Veteran*, liberated by a French Privateer in Martinique Jun 1747, *P.3.346, MR.207, CA.3.132, PRO.SP36.102.ff.120r-121v*

STEWART, JOHN, aged 17, labourer in Perthshire, imprisoned in Lancaster Castle, transported to Antigua 8.5.1747 *P.3.346*

STEWART, JOHN, of Glat, parish of Callander, carried arms, whereabouts not known *SHS.8.60*

STEWART, JOHN, brewer, Collingtowngill, parish of Callander, whereabouts not known *SHS.8.60*

STEWART, JOHN, from Balquhidder, in Glengyle's Regiment, imprisoned 5.7.1746 Perth, 10.8.1746 Canongate, discharged on bail 30.9.1746, "common man" *P.3.346*

STEWART, LAURENCE, cook and tailor, Dunkeld, now at home *CA.3.306, SHS.8.52*

STEWART, MALCOLM, Lieutenant, brother to Shierglas, parish of Mullion, Atholl Brigade, now lurking in the hills *CA.3.302, SHS.8.50, MR.20*

STEWART, NEIL, Captain, of Temper, Atholl Brigade, killed, Culloden *CA.3.298, CA.3.302, CA.3.308, MR.19*

STEWART, PATRICK, Captain, of Easter Invervack, Atholl Brigade, taken prisoner, tried, found guilty, recommended to mercy *CA.3.302, CA.3.308, MR.19*

STEWART, PATRICK, Captain, Innerslanie, Atholl Brigade, *CA.3.302, MR.19*

STEWART, PATRICK, labourer, Innerbaik, Perthshire, Tullibardine's (ie Duke of Atholl's) Regiment, surrendered 22.7.1746 imprisoned Perth, 10.8.1746 Canongate, Carlisle, pardoned on condition of enlistment 22.7.1748. Was tried 19 Sept 1746 and sentenced to death, but recommended to mercy by the Jury. He appealed against having to enlist on the ground that he had been forced *P.3.348*

STEWART, ROBERT, Captain, Mains of Lude, Atholl Brigade, commanding Lude Company *CA.3.302, MR.19*

STEWART, ROBERT, Major, of Killiechassie, parish of Weem, 4th Battalion, Atholl Brigade, commanding his own tenants, now lurking in hills *CA.3.302, CA.3.308, SHS.8.50, MR.21*

STEWART, ROBERT (ANDREW?), younger of Ballechin, Officer, Atholl Brigade, *CA.3.302, CA.3.308, MR.21*

STEWART, ROBERT, servant, Dunkeld, prisoner in Perth prison *CA.3.306, SHS.8.52*

STEWART, ROBERT, Dunkeld, labourer *CA.3.307*

STEWART, THOMAS, of Wester Kinnaird, cottar, Atholl Brigade (paid listing money), at Culloden *CA.3.304, MR.28*

STEWART, THOMAS, Mickleour, servant to Aldie, 3rd Battalion, Atholl Brigade, pardoned *MR.28*

STEWART, THOMAS, aged 19 from Perth, Duke of Perth's Regiment, imprisoned Lancaster, transported 1747. No further reference to him *P.3.348*

STEWART, WALTER, Captain, of Orchil Beag Atholl Brigade, *CA.3.302, MR.19*

STEWART, WILLIAM, Captain, of Garth, parish of Dull, Atholl Brigade, commanded his own tenants, now lurking in the hills *CA.3.302, CA.3.308, SHS.8.50, MR.19*

STEWART, WILLIAM, brother of Captain William Stewart of Garth, Officer, now lurking in the hills *CA.3.303, SHS.8.50*

STEWART, WILLIAM, aged 19, Perthshire, 1st Battalion, Atholl Brigade, taken prisoner, died *MR.28*

STEWART, WILLIAM, Drummond, parish of Muthill, carried arms as a volunteer, whereabouts not known *SHS.8.50*

STIRLING, GEORGE, surgeon from Perth, imprisoned 7.2.1746 Perth, 1.4.1746 Edinburgh, discharged on bail 20.6.1746. "Suspicion of treason." *P.3.248*

STIRLING, JAMES, merchant from Perth, imprisoned 7.2.1746 Perth, 1.4.1746 Edinburgh Jail from the Castle, liberated 20.6.1746 *P.3.350*

STRATHALLAN, Lady MARGARET, Strathallan, Perthshire, imprisoned Strathallan House, 11.2.1746 Edinburgh Castle, liberated 22.11.1746 on bail. "Subsists herself." Edinburgh Castle. Margaret, daughter of William, second Lord Nairn, was the wife of William, Viscount of Strathallan. For her active support of the Prince she was on 11 Feb 1746 committed to Edinburgh Castle, and remained there until 22.11.1746, when she was liberated on bail. "Witnesses say they frequently saw her drink the Pretender's health and success to his arms in Britain and said that she put out illuminations on the Pretender's birthday in a most remarkable manner." *P.3.354*

STRATHALLAN, Lord, Machony, parish of Muthill, whereabouts not known *SHS.8.50*

STRATHALLAN, Viscount of, Colonel, Perthshire Horse, killed at Culloden *MR.53*

SYME, THOMAS, Mr, nonjurant Preacher, Ardgath, parish of Errol, Perthshire, "carried arms and went north with the rebels," returned and is now lurking *SHS.8.236*

SYME, THOMAS, workman, Sea Side, parish of Errol, Perthshire, "carried arms and was at the battle of Falkirk with the rebels, but wrong in his judgement," returned and is now lurking *SHS.8.236*

TAYLOR, GEORGE, Muthill, Perthshire, Duke of Perth's Regiment, imprisoned Muthill, 23.3.1746 Stirling, Edinburgh, discharged 17.7.1747. "Hireman to Duke of Perth." "On suspicion." "Witnesses declared he was seen driving the rebels' cannon wearing the white cockade. After the battle of Falkirk was seen riding a dragoon horse, armed with pistols, with a dragoon cloak about him." *P.3.364, MR.76*

THOMSON, JAMES, gardener in Fingask, parish of Kinnaird, Perthshire, carried arms and went with the army to England and was taken prisoner at Carlisle 30.12.1745 *SHS.8.238*

THOMSON, JAMES, tenant in Potthill, volunteer, prisoner at Stirling, transported *SHS.8.52, MR.69*

THOMSON, ROBERT, tenant farmer in Potthill, Perth, volunteer in Duke of Perth's Regiment, prisoner at Stirling, released under General pardon, 1747 *SHS.8.52, P.3.372, MR.76*

THREEPLAND, THOMAS, Captain, son to Sir David of Fingask, parish of Kinnaird, Perthshire, at the battle of Preston and killed there *SHS.8.238*

TOSHACK, DAVID, a butcher in Perth, imprisoned in Perth and Edinburgh, released. "He took part in the guarding of the prisoners captured at the taking of the *Hazard*." When confined in Perth prison he mentioned that he had seen the Earl of Cromarty mustering his men and he was then ordered to be sent to London. He decided, however, to retract his statement when he appeared before the Lord Justice Clerk. He was accordingly released *P.3.374*

TULLIBARDINE, Marquis of WILLIAM MURRAY (Jacobite Duke of Atholl), aged 58, Perthshire, surrendered 27.4.1746, imprisoned April 1746 Dumbarton, Leith, shipped on *HMS Eltham* June 1746 Tower of London, died in Tower 9.7.1746. He was second son of John, 1st Duke of Atholl, and was born 14 Apr 1689. On his elder brother's death he became Marquis of Tullibardine. In 1715 he joined the Earl of Mar and commanded a regiment of the Atholl Brigade, and acted as Lieutenant-General at Sheriffmuir. In consequence of this he was attainted on 19 Feb 1716 but escaped to France. He was appointed in 1717 by James VIII to the chief command in Scotland, and on 1 Feb was created Jacobite Duke of Rannoch. He accompanied the Spanish force in 1719 and was defeated at Glenshiel on 10 June. A large reward was offered for his apprehension, but he again escaped to France and there lived in straitened circumstances. He returned to Scotland with the Prince in July 1745. He then assumed the title of Duke of Atholl and took possession of the estates. After Culloden, being in bad health, he sought shelter in Dumbartonshire at Drumakill, where, according to Bishop Forbes, he was betrayed by his host, Buchanan of Drumakill, and was arrested and put in Dumbarton Castle. Thence he was sent to London on 20 June 1746 and was confined in the Tower. He died on 9 July 1746, and was buried in the

Tower Chapel. An obituary notice, describing his illness, appears in the *Scots Mag* of July 1746 *P.3.378*

TURNBULL, JOHN, servant to Mr William Keir, merchant, Perth, imprisoned Feb 1746 Perth, 30.3.1746 Edinburgh, released under General Pardon, 1747. "On suspicion." *P.3.380*

URQUHART, GEORGE, in Ballinluig, cottar, Atholl Brigade, (paid listing money), at Culloden *CA.3.303, MR.28*

WADDELL, JOHN, Perthshire, in French Service, imprisoned 13.12.1745 Edinburgh Royal Infirmary, released under General Pardon, 1747. The Jail return shows him as a "French deserter." He probably came over with the French troops *P.3.384*

WALLACE, JOHN, in Ballintuim, at Culloden, Atholl Brigade, (paid listing money) *CA.3.305, MR.28*

WARDEN, JAMES, schoolmaster from Alyth, Perthshire, imprisoned 1.7.1746 Perth, discharged 9.7.1746. On suspicion. "Thomas Mathew did hear him drink the Pretender's son's health by the name of Prince Charles. Witnesses declare that he sang treasonable songs and uttered treasonable words." *P.3.388*

WHITE, JAMES, victualler, Meigle, Perthshire, "kept a Court as Barron Baillie which he caused fence in the Pretender's name as James the 8th King of Great Brittain, etc, and was very active in serving their interest," now at home *SHS.8.240*

WHITE, ROBERT, painter from Glasgow, born 28.9.1718, son of James White and Jane Selkrig, served in Duke of Perth's Regiment, Atholl Brigade, transported 1747, *P.3.400, CA.3.306, MR.77*

WHYTE, NICCOL, Perthshire, "in rebel service," imprisoned 13.6.1746 Perth, hanged 31.7.1746. Deserter from the army *P.3.400*

WILL, JAMES, wright, Meigle, Perthshire, carried arms and went to England with the Rebels, was taken prisoner at Carlisle 30.12.1745 *SHS.8.242*

WILL (or WILLS), WILLIAM, Meigle, Perthshire, Ogilvy's Regiment, imprisoned 30.12.1745 Carlisle, York Castle. Captured at the surrender of Carlisle to Cumberland. Disposal unknown. Name not on transportation lists *P.3.402*

WILLS, WILLIAM, Sergeant, Meigle, Perthshire, Ogilvy's Regiment, imprisoned 30.12.1745 Carlisle, Southwark, discharged. Taken at capture of Carlisle. He gave evidence against Charles Gordon, younger of Binhall, at his trial at Southwark *P.3.404*

WILSON, DAVID, resident of Scone, armed and in a mob at Perth on the anniversary of His Majesty's birthday, went north with the rebels *SHS.8.52*

WILSON, JAMES, Atholl, Perthshire, 3rd Battalion, Duke of Atholl's Regiment, imprisoned 27.1.1746 Edinburgh, released under General Pardon, 1747 "a common highlander" on suspicion *P.3.404, MR.28*

WRIGHT, DANIEL, Thornhill, 3rd Battalion, Atholl Brigade, taken prisoner 2.2.1746, pardoned *MR.28*

YOUNG, DAVID, weaver in Newbiggin, Newtyle parish, Perthshire, carried arms, being hired by the country, was at Inverury skirmish and after that surrendered himself, now at home *SHS.8.242*

YOUNG, ROBERT, resident of Coupar Angus, Perthshire, carried arms and was at the battle of Falkirk and after that at home *MR.113, SHS.8.242*

YOULLY, DAVID, weaver at Newbiggin, parish of Newtyle, Perthshire, carried arms, being hired by the country, was at Inverury skirmish and after that surrendered himself, now at home *SHS.8.242*

YUILL, JAMES, horse hirer, living in Bridgend, Kinnoull, Perth, imprisoned Perth 13.2.1746, 30.3.1746 Edinburgh, released under General Pardon, 1747. "Confessed he bore arms on 30 Oct last." On suspicion. "Appeared in arms in a mob at Perth on the anniversary of His Majesty's birthday." *SHS.8.52, P.3.412*

Frances McDonnell Publications

ABERDEEN OBITUARIES
- 1748-1770
- 1771-1799
- 1800-1822
- 1823-1839
- 1840-1854

ALUMNI & GRADUATES IN ARTS OF THE ABERDEEN COLLEGES
- 1850-1860
- 1840-1849

BIRTH BRIEFS OF ABERDEEN 1637-1705

THE BURGESS ROLL OF BANFF

THE BURGESS ROLL OF ELGIN

BURGH OF PAISLEY POLL TAX ROLL 1695
- Part 1
- Part 2

GENERAL REGISTER OF SASINES
- County of Aberdeen 1701-1720
- Counties of Banff, Elgin, Forres, Nairn & Kincardine 1701-20

JACOBITES OF 1715, NORTH EAST SCOTLAND

JACOBITES OF 1745, NORTH EAST SCOTLAND

REGISTER OF MERCHANT AND TRADE BURGESSES OF ABERDEEN
- Part 1 1600-1620
- Part 2 1621-1639
- Part 3 1640-1659
- Part 4 1660-1679
- Part 5 1680-1700

REGISTER OF MERCHANT AND TRADE BURGESSES OF OLD ABERDEEN
- Part 1 1605-1725
- Part 2 1726-1885

ROLL OF APPRENTICES, BURGH OF ABERDEEN
- Part 1 1622-1699
- Part 2 1700-1750
- Part 3 1751-1796

REGISTER OF TESTAMENTS, ABERDEEN
- 1760-1800
- 1735-1759
- 1715-1734

SCOTTISH CATHOLIC PARENTS AND THEIR CHILDREN 1701–1705

THE ADVENTURES OF PETER WILLIAMSON
(32 page illustrated booklet)
Child abduction in Aberdeen, for sale into slavery on the American plantations

EMIGRANTS FROM IRELAND TO AMERICA, 1735-1743
Published by and available from Genealogical Publishing Co Inc, Baltimore, Maryland,

CPSIA information can be obtained
at www.ICGtesting.com
Printed in the USA
BVHW071356051119
562966BV00015B/169/P